A Better
Admissions Test

Raising the Standard for College Entrance Exams

Distributed from Baton Rouge, Louisiana by Mud House Art and Literature. Mud House Art and Literature is a nonprofit distributor of visual art, original literature, and literature in the public domain.

Project Managers: Jeremy Tate and Brian G. Daigle
General Editor: Brian G. Daigle
Editor: Julie Dreher
Page design by Brian G. Daigle
Cover design by Brian G. Daigle
Cover art: "Young Scholar in his Study" by Pieter Codde (c.1630-5)

Mud House Art and Literature titles may be purchased in bulk for educational, business, fund-raising, or sales promotional use. For information, please email MudHouseArt@gmail.com

Printed in the United States of America

For the educator who knows there's another way.

Table of Contents

Introduction
Brian G. Daigle

As a student moves into their grammar or elementary school years, whether educated at home or in a traditional setting, a good formal education must look beyond itself; it must look at a broader, more final goal of education. For some students, the road to this final goal will include college. For others, college will not be the best option. Either way, a student ought to receive a good general K–12 education in order to provide him with the best options when leaving high school. Even if college is in the cards, a good college education will look beyond itself, even beyond mere job placement. Therefore, a good K–12 education is much more than college preparation.

Along with being well acquainted with the best literature, ideas, academic advances, scholarly disciplines, and challenges in one's tradition, a good education means a student learns to master the most important and most basic academic disciplines: reading, writing, speaking, thinking, and listening. Specifically, many curricula have required credit hours in order to achieve the highest academic standards possible. It is important that each credit hour a student takes contributes to the best education a student can receive, whether or not that student plans to enroll in an institution of higher learning. As a student matures, the standard of education should mature with him. As a student moves closer to making a decision about life after high school, his academic work should begin to focus within a certain vocation or academic field, making sure not to neglect the other academic disciplines which will make for an *actual* education. A focus on having a high standard in the right areas will inevitably lead to a student's success on lower planes, like standardized tests. This book exists because there is not only a specific need to reform standards of standardized tests; there is a broader need to reform standards of education in general. If our students are to succeed at a particular test, and if that test is to be worth its salt, then our education principles and practices in general ought to be worthy of our time and resources. In an attempt to mature our education principles and practices, and therefore to make sure our tests are worthy to be called the *standard*, this book has three divisions.

Part one is called "Setting the Stage." These chapters have a certain revelatory quality, a quality which shows the reader our scaffolding, our blueprints, the materials and engineering decisions which hold up the whole building. More than that, the chapters in the first part offer a way for the reader to see the paradigms by which the ideas in this book function. If we are going to ask what kind of tests a human should take, then we should start by first understanding what a human is.

Part two is called "Questioning the Standard." These chapters will be more critical, assessing, questioning, and poking the principles and practices that have given us our current standards in college entrance exams specifically and higher academic studies in general. If these chapters have their intended effect, the reader should walk away disillusioned by what many of us for decades have held up as the standard for college entrance. In the least, we will see the rationale for an alternative.

Part three is called "Tests Have Consequences." If we see in part two of this book that tests have premises, then part three should show us that tests likewise have consequences—they have both intended and unintended fruit, broadly and locally. Students are formed by tests. Schools oftentimes reflect the shape of the tests they give their students. Some teachers even plan their entire scope and sequence around the presence and particulars of a test. State and federal education laws are passed because researchers squeeze out enough data points from standardized testing. If we plan on replacing a grotesque and badly broken academic model by replacing the foundation, then we must recognize the consequences resulting from our current model, and we must know the consequences of any other foundation we intend to lay.

Most books like this attempt to deal in terms of superficial particulars. That is, if a standardized test were a cathedral, commonplace discussion would debate window dressings and gargoyle expressions. At the outset, it must be stated that this book fights on different ground. The authors here may go so far as to question the very purpose of the cathedral. We may even ask the reader to consider if the best word for such a structure is *cathedral*. It is one thing to change the color of the Italian stone—having four multiple choice answers instead of five. It is quite another to commission a German architect to do the job in Tokyo.

Along the same lines, the reader will notice that many of the ideas presented here have prescriptions and conclusions wholly different from what one finds in today's academic institutions. If you were expecting Italian stone, the Japanese wood may surprise you. This is no accident. Each conclusion given here—set at odds with today's academic practices and principles—has arisen because of an entirely different starting point. A man may want to travel on foot from Rio to Rome, but his starting point has eliminated any possibility of making it to Rome by his desired transportation. A walking path to Rome will not be found within this man's continental starting point. A man who begins in Rio, therefore, should plan, at best, to make his bed in Raleigh, if he has the legs to leap over the Darien Gap. Alternatively, if a man awakens in Raleigh, we are confident he did not walk from Rome. If this book builds a different school from the one where we were educated, it's because it has started from a different worldview, perhaps altogether at a different continental point of origin.

Not only does this book fight on different ground, it may be said to fight *beneath* the ground. If the ideas here seem foundational, they are; they have been written for a time such as ours, a time which sorely needs a reconsideration of our presuppositions—academic and otherwise. If the chapters seem philosophical, they are because the authors have sought wisdom. If the paradigm seems religious, it is because we couldn't help ourselves. If at any point while reading these chapters, the reader accuses us of being too religious, not giving enough space between our theory of education and our religious doctrine, and therefore being too religious in our academic sentiments and educational direction, I can only say he is right. And I can only say he would be more accurate to charge us with being too honest. For if I am commissioned with the task of compiling a recipe book of the best Italian cuisine, and I believe no other city than Florence can give us the recipes we need, then I would be remiss to fill the pages with dishes from Rome, Naples, Venice, or Milan. And I would certainly not fill the pages with dishes from Moscow. I would wear the Florentine badge proudly, because I would at least be wearing it honestly. And if I was correct that Florence had the best Italian cuisine, then I would wear the badge with great conviction and without shame. And I would certainly ask you why you aren't wearing yours. Thus, the ideas which fill these pages are decidedly religious, because they reflect their authors. I would be surprised if my secular friend's own book on standards in education and testing had the same ideas, for then his book wouldn't be worth reading. I would know from the outset that he was a fraud. I would know he had first lied to himself about his own convictions, and therefore would not bat an eye at lying to his reader. I would therefore know he was not a worthy partner for debate, for he did not quite know where he stood and the implications of his position. And this means I would know a very untrustworthy teacher had, ironically, compiled a book about education standards. I would dismiss him with all the other sophists in history. We stand in a long tradition of scholars, scientists, theologians, poets, and priests. In that long line there are a select few, called moderns, who exist in a small bit of history. These few have sought a revolution, an overthrow—truly a throwing out and purgation—of their academic parents and cultural traditions. *Hubris* cast in a Broadway musical may look like Dewey or Derrida; when flattened and printed, *hubris* most certainly will be placed in front of high school seniors as the standard for answering the question, "What must I do, professor, to be collegiate?" The history of standardized testing is set: ideas have driven decisions which have had bad consequences, intended or unintended. But the future of standardized testing is still up for grabs. True progress in higher education must call for a reform of college entrance exams; perhaps we would be so courageous as to ask for a renaissance.

Part I

Setting the Stage

1

A Brief History

Daniel Foucachon

Daniel Foucachon grew up in Lyon, France where his father was an evangelist and church-planter with Mission to the World. He moved to Moscow, Idaho in 2005 to attend New Saint Andrews College, where he graduated with a BA in Liberal Arts and Culture in 2009. In 2009 he founded a media production company, and was the producer of Canon Wired (the media branch of Canon Press) until 2013. His love for classical education and desire to publish curriculum designed for home education led him to found Roman Roads Media in 2011, which has since produced and published award-winning liberal arts curriculum for high school students. He and his wife Lydia live in Moscow, Idaho with their three sons and one daughter.

Carl Brigham created the SAT examination based on World War I IQ tests. It was administered for the first time in the Fall of 1926. A mere eleven years later, a distraught yet wiser Brigham wrote, "It is probably simpler to teach cultured men testing than to give testers culture." Concerned with the direction of his own early work in standardized testing, he held back the advance of standardized exams until his death in 1943. This was a turning point in the history of education in the United States.

Entrance Exams Before America

Throughout antiquity, education was a very personal enterprise. There were few if any exams for entrance to schools at any level, much less anything resembling our modern standardized exams. This continued through the Roman period and into the Middle Ages, where education was most often organized and supervised by the Church (typically the local church, meaning it differed from region to region). Most education was oriented toward career students of some sort (teachers or clergy), or toward nobility and those whose vocation was governing and managing lands, towns, and people. As such, entrance to a school was more a question of position in society than one of knowledge or aptitude.

As Europe moved away from the feudal system and became more politically unified, many areas of life and culture began to follow this unification, including schools and universities; as a consequence a need for collaboration emerged. The first sparks of the Protestant Reformation began in the twelfth century among the Waldensians, who insisted on the necessity of the Scriptures in the common tongue. As their ideas kindled, culminating in the Reformation of the sixteenth century, the educational landscape changed. Where education had been emphasized primarily among clergy and nobility in leadership, now basic literacy (at a minimum) was expected among every worshipper of God. It was during the Reformation, partly under the influence of Luther and Calvin, that teacher certifications were first set in place. The expectation of universal literacy came to the New World, so that years later John Adams, the second president of the United States (in a dissertation discussing the American emphasis on schools and education), made the comment that an illiterate American is as "rare as a comet."

This basic, almost universal literacy is the backdrop to the founding of universities in America in the seventeenth century. While entrance exams as we know them today had not yet been established, expectations of what a student would know when entering a university were more or less set. Building upon the literacy expected of every man, an educated (university-bound) student was expected to have the foundation of a *liberal arts education*. A "liberal arts" education can be defined as the education suited to a free man based in the first principles of the Western tradition. There are two aspects to this liberal arts education: the liberal or free nature of the education, which has to do with "who" and "why," and its content, the "arts" of the free man. In order to understand the redefinition of education that happened at the beginning of the twentieth century, we have to understand what education meant for the preceding centuries.

Liberal

The word *liberal* has nothing to do with our common use of the word in politics and culture. Liberal means "free," and historically described the kind of education expected of a freeman--especially one in a position of leadership, like the nobility. What distinguishes an education of a "free man" and that of a non-free man, that of a vassal or serf or slave? After all, 2 + 2 = 4, and both a freeman and a vassal would need to know that. Our culture has so alienated itself from a historic education that it's very difficult for us to think of education proper, and *not* to jump to the practical and objective aspect of education. When we think of education, we think of jobs and vocational training.

Dr. Roy Atwood, founding president of New Saint Andrews College (a classical liberal arts college in Moscow, Idaho that follows the old Harvard model of education) tells of the time he was asked by a student,

"Who are you"? His automatic response was to give his profession: "Uh...I'm a professor." But the student responded, "No, I don't mean what you do, but who are you?" We are programmed to answer that question with what we do, with our job title. We think of education in terms of answering the question, "Will this degree or college prepare me for a job?" We have received this faulty understanding of education fairly recently. But the modern definition of education does more; it not only defines education in terms of usefulness, but in so doing defines human beings by our usefulness as well. This indoctrination starts at a young age. If you have young children, you may have sat with them and watched *Thomas the Tank Engine.* Have you noticed that in that children's program the child's entire worth is summed up in terms of how *useful* they are? "You're a useful little train, Thomas." These anthropomorphic characters tell our children a story, and instill at a very young age that our purpose as human beings is to be "useful." Consequently, our children are not surprised as teenagers when they are told to think about college, or pressed for what major they will pursue, and much more importantly, what kind of job they think that degree will give them. And that job will define them. "I am a professor," or "I am a dentist."

Christians of previous generations viewed education, and themselves, differently. The opening lines of the *Westminster Shorter Catechism* would have been familiar to nearly every school-aged student in the New World: "The chief end of man is to glorify God and enjoy him forever." That is who we are: worshipping beings who delight in God. Or to use Dr. Atwood's answer to the question "who are you?": we are royalty, heirs of Christ. And we should educate our children as royalty in Christ.

Some may object that this identity has nothing to do with education. The founders of Harvard College would disagree. These are the "Rules and Precepts" of Harvard College, written shortly after its founding in 1646, defining precisely what education was all about:

> Let every Student be plainly instructed, and earnestly pressed to consider well, the maine end of his life and studies is, to know God and Jesus Christ which is eternal life (John 17:3) and therefore to lay Christ in the bottome, as the only foundation of all sound knowledge and Learning. And seeing the Lord only giveth wisdom, Let every one seriously set himself by prayer in secret to seeke it of him (Prov. 2:3).

To know Christ, and to make Him the foundation. Christ is both the source and the goal of education.

"Who are you?" Our answer should be that we are free (liberal) Christians, pursuing wisdom and virtue through the interwoven arts of theology (study of the knowledge of God) and humanities (study of ourselves and of mankind). "Knowledge of God and knowledge of self," which is how John Calvin sets the stage for his *Institutes of the Christian Religion*, is also how Harvard and other universities in the United States prior to the 1900s set the foundation for education.

The Arts

The term "liberal" points to the purpose of education and our identity, but does not answer the practical question of what this looks like. What are these "arts"? If classical education is an education in first principles, then what are those first principles?

If you've read much on classical education, then the *trivium* and *quadrivium* (the seven liberal arts inherited from antiquity and developed in the Medieval period) may come to mind. A common objection is to ask why this period gets special treatment. The answer begins by returning to our assumption that education begins with knowledge of God and knowledge of self. If we are to know God properly, we must study his Word, the history of His people, and ourselves. The Western heritage of the classical liberal arts is not a Western privilege or elitism. It is the common inheritance of all God's people. It is the cultural soil into which Christ was made flesh. It was also the culture in which the Church grew. And it has been carried and preserved by Christians for 2000 years. Starting with the Apostle Paul, and continuing through the period of the early church fathers, the Reformers, and all our American founding fathers–they all had in common a classical liberal arts education. We as a people are the product of this Western thought. In short, a liberal arts education *is* an education in first principles. This means an education which includes Plato and Aristotle, Aquinas and Dante, Augustine and Boethius, Cicero and Plutarch, Homer and Vergil, Milton and Shakespeare. It is a study of ourselves, and where we came from. We may have only recently rediscovered this birthright, but it is not presumptuous to receive this heritage as our own.

The founders of Harvard College demonstrate the devotion to the liberal arts in their early entrance examinations. Remember the goal of education that Harvard laid out, stated earlier, to "lay Christ at the bottom." How did they expect their entering students to be equipped for this task?

In his *Three Centuries of Harvard*, Samuel Morison describes their early entrance exams:

> The earliest entrance requirements were extempore translation of Cicero and the ability to write and speak Latin *suo ut aiunt Marte* (by one's own skill), and a little Greek grammar.

Jumping ahead a few years, we can observe a more extensive example of this in the Harvard entrance exam of 1869. Here are a few example questions, as they were stated on the exam, from the *History and Geography* portion:

4. Describe the route of the Ten Thousand, or lay it down on a map.
5. Leonidas, Pausanias, Lysander.
6. Pharsalia, Philippi, Actium, — geographically and historically.
8. Compare Athens with Sparta
9. Pericles: the Man and his Policy.

And a longer question:

7. Supply the two names left blank in the following passage from the Oration for the Manilian Law: Non dicam duas urbes potentissimas, *Carthaginem* et *Numantiam* ab eodem _____ esse deletas; non commemorabo nuper ita vobis patribusque esse visum, ut in uno _____ spes imperii poneretur, ut idem cum *Jugurtha*, idem cum *Cimbris*, idem cum *Teutonis* bellum administraret." Who was Jugurtha? Where was Numantia?

Notice two things. First, like a well-worn joke which evokes laughter at the mere mention of the first line, the ideas represented on the exam were expected to be so familiar to these college applicants that the mere mention of single words was all that was needed to prompt a student to write an essay about their significance. Leonidas is the author of the phrase "molon labe" or "come and take them," when he and his 300 men refused to surrender their weapons and held the entire Persian army at bay in a narrow pass at Thermopylae, fighting to the death. That one name would prompt an answer by a student, an essay which could include the actual story, but also ethics, philosophy, theology, or morality. These stories and ideas were the common possession of the educated American.

Second, notice the longer example in Latin! This is *not* the language or Latin portion of the exam. It was expected that the student could converse fluently in Latin. We tend to marvel at the fluency required of these students, when our focus is merely on the language skill itself. But while this is impressive, and the knowledge of the grammar and vocabulary of these languages was an important part of their education, what is more remarkable is the content. They were not translating random texts to illustrate their mastery of the language, but demonstrating their use of Latin *as a tool* to interact with the ancient texts. In other words, the expectation of a student entering higher education was that he possessed the tools of learning, and knew how to apply those tools to the subject at hand: grappling with the ideas of "old Western culture," as C.S. Lewis describes it. They had the tools to fulfill the definition of education given by G.K. Chesterton, who said that "education is simply the soul of a society as it passes from one generation to another." It was an education in the first principles of the West—*a classical liberal arts education.*

This was what education looked like in America until the early 1900s. What happened after that point?

The Redefinition of Education and the Advent of the SAT
The "college boards," introduced in 1900, were a series of essay examinations lasting an entire week. These exams thoroughly covered the knowledge one was expected to have when entering college, very much in line with the expectations of the past several hundred years. If you are familiar with *Anne of Avonlea*, you may recall an important part of the story involves the "boards" examinations that Anne is required to take. She studies extensively, and then goes to take them over several days. These exams were unique in that they represented a more standardized exam than had previously existed, monitored by the College Entrance Examination Board rather than by individual colleges. And for prestigious colleges they were the primary entrance exam until a precise date. On December 7, 1941, the Japanese bombed Pearl Harbor. "Within two weeks, the essay exams had been suspended for the durations of the war," writes Lemann in *The Big Test*; "They were never resumed." He continues:

So all that had to happen was for the United
States to enter the war–and the SAT immediately
became the admissions device for the most
prestigious private colleges in the country,
something that would previously have been an
unthinkably radical step.

The SAT was developed by Carl Brigham, a Princeton
professor, who was involved with the research from IQ
testing of World War I soldiers. In 1923 Brigham wrote
about his results in a book, *A Study of American
Intelligence,* in which he "trafficked in the prevailing
eugenicist theory of the day," concluding that certain
races were more intelligent than others, and that
American intelligence was declining as the result of
mixing races. As the war ended he took what he learned
from the Army IQ tests and turned his attention to
education. In 1926, using the standardized exam format
recently developed by Frederick J. Kelly, he upgraded the
exam to suit the university context and wrote the
Scholastic Aptitude Test, the SAT. As Lemann remarks,
it has changed remarkably little since then.

Instead of examining knowledge and one's ability
to use the tools of learning, the SAT now measured for
intelligence. Peter Sacks, in his book *Standardized Minds,*
explains how this shift to measuring IQ influenced our
culture. We began to look for "potential" instead of

experience or knowledge; we started to measure aptitude instead of accomplishment. Sacks wrote that "promoters of the IQ test succeeded in convincing policymakers and the public that the intelligence test amounted to a final, indisputable measurement of human performance." The SAT exam was an attempt to create a more pure class of intellectual elites. But it was thoroughly flawed because it was based on the assumption that intelligence was a biological trait, connected with race. Interestingly, the creator of the SAT soon become one of its harshest critics. The more Carl Brigham was involved in the development of standardized testing, the more he pushed back, even formally retracting his previous bestseller, *A Study of American Intelligence*, calling it "pretentious" and "without foundation," and attempting to distance the SAT (which he still considered of value) from IQ testing. It came to the point that Brigham was the sole roadblock to the formation of a new, unified testing agency which would combine all the exams under one banner.

Brigham wrote a critical (and eerily prophetic) letter to James Bryant Conant. Conant, president of Harvard at the time, was pushing for this unified testing agency, but more importantly for using the SAT to create a new elite based on intelligence, while (in his words) "wielding the axe against the root of inherited privilege."

If the unhappy day ever comes when teachers point their students toward these newer examinations, and the present weak and restricted procedures get a grip on education, then we may look for the inevitable distortion of education in the terms of tests. And that means that mathematics will continue to be completely departmentalized and broken into disintegrated bits, that the sciences will become highly verbalized and the computation, manipulation and thinking in terms other than verbal will be minimized, that languages will be taught for linguistic skills only without reference to literary values, that English will be taught for reading alone, and that practice and drill in writing of English will disappear.

While attempting to create a tool to select America's elites, the SAT actually changed the nature of education. It led not to the cultivation of individuals, but the development of assets of the state. It answers the question, "In which station will you best fit in society?" That is not the proper purpose of education. If a student is going to be an effective member of society, he must have an education in first principles of that society. Our children are not cogs in a statist machine, or lab rats in a social experiment. In his later years Brigham saw this danger stating, "A college being a humanitarian institution cannot afford to make mistakes against the individual."

Frederick J. Kelly, who in 1914 invented the standardized exam format which Brigham used for the SAT, has a similar story. After his work developing standardized testing he too saw the danger it posed to the proper understanding of education. In his inaugural address as President of the University of Idaho in 1928, Kelly stated that "College is a place to learn how to educate oneself rather than a place in which to be educated." In other words, education is about the tools of learning, or as he put it, education "should be confined to those fundamentals which serve best as a basis for subsequent learning." Following these convictions, Kelly implemented a two year, unified liberal arts curriculum at the University of Idaho. He was removed from office two years later, in 1930. His primary goal as president was to go against the system he helped create, but his efforts were not appreciated.

Conclusion

The shift represented by the advent of the SAT exam is a change in the purpose of education from cultivating a worshiping being to developing assets. Instead of evaluating students on the dangerous tools of grammar (language and words), logic (critical thinking), and rhetoric (eloquence and persuasion), the modern testing system is a curator of assets, batch-testing for intelligence and aptitude. As Dr. Roy Atwood points out in a future chapter, recent changes to the SAT indicate a past failure of correctly evaluating a student's education, and do not instill confidence in its future any more than its past.

As Christian parents and educators across the country continue to revive classical learning in our homes and schools, we are beginning to see a generation of well-equipped, culturally and professionally engaged students steeped in the liberal arts who are seeking higher education. And as institutions of higher learning are seeking such students, the need for a new and better kind of entrance exam is obvious, because modern standardized exams have failed us.

The Classical Learning Test (CLT) is a countering step, acting against a culture which has not only redefined education, but tried to redefine us as humans. It allows students to pursue *true* education and to be examined on that basis. It offers institutions of higher learning a way to measure the knowledge of students in the liberal arts, and to see whether they possess the tools to make that knowledge dangerous to a secular world.

2

Homo Viator vs. Homo Superbus: G.K. Chesterton and Modern Education

Joseph Pearce

A native of England, Joseph Pearce is Director of the Center for Faith and Culture at Aquinas College in Nashville, Tennessee. He is editor of the *St. Austin Review*, series editor of the Ignatius Critical Editions, and executive director of Catholic Courses. He is the author of many books, including studies of Shakespeare, Tolkien, C. S. Lewis, Oscar Wilde, and G. K. Chesterton. His books have been published and translated into Spanish, Portuguese, French, Dutch, Italian, Korean, Mandarin, Croatian, and Polish. Pearce has hosted two 13-part television series about Shakespeare on EWTN, and has also written and presented documentaries on EWTN on the Catholicism of *The Lord of the Rings* and *The Hobbit*. He has participated and lectured at a wide variety of international and literary events at major colleges and universities in the U.S., Canada, Britain, Europe, Africa, and South America. Joseph is a regular guest on national television and radio programs, and has served as consultant for film documentaries on J.R.R. Tolkien, Francis Thompson, and Alexander Solzhenitsyn.

Gilbert Keith Chesterton is one of the giants of the twentieth century. As a novelist, his reputation is assured through the idiosyncratic splendor of works such as *The Man Who was Thursday* and *The Ball and the Cross*; as a poet, he is rightly esteemed for *The Ballad of the White Horse* and for the eulogizing of one of Christendom's finest hours in "Lepanto"; and as a Christian apologist in works such as *Orthodoxy* and *The Everlasting Man* he has been instrumental in influencing the conversion of many of the century's finest writers, including C.S. Lewis. As a wit, he was a match for Oscar Wilde and George Bernard Shaw. To Oscar Wilde's statement that we cannot appreciate sunsets because we cannot pay for them, Chesterton's riposte was that Oscar Wilde could pay for sunsets by not being Oscar Wilde.[1] Similarly, he was asked following a speech on "The Coming Peril" whether he considered Bernard Shaw a "coming peril." "Heavens, no," Chesterton replied, "he is a disappearing pleasure."[2] Shaw, in turn, referred to Chesterton as "a colossal genius."[3]

Yet it was not in the speed of his wit but in the depth of his philosophy that his true genius resided.

---

[1] W. R. Titterton, *G. K. Chesterton: A Portrait*, London: Alexander Ouseley Ltd, 1936, pp. 88-9
[2] Maisie Ward, *Gilbert Keith Chesterton*, London: Sheed & Ward, 1944, p. 501
[3] Christopher Hollis, *The Mind of Chesterton*, London: Hollis & Carter, 1970, p. 86

Chesterton was, in the literal sense of the word, a radical thinker. He went back to the very roots of a problem in order to understand it and solve it. "The modern man," he wrote, "is more like a traveller who has forgotten the name of his destination, and has to go back whence he came, even to find out where he is going."[4] The problem, however, is that modern man does not even know that he is a traveller. He is unaware that he is on a journey or that he has a destination. He is not *homo viator*,[5] nor is he *homo sapiens*, in the sense that he does not even know the difference between sapience and techne, or between wisdom and knowledge. In truth, modern man, and still more postmodern man, [6] is *homo superbus*, a pathetic creature who is trapped within the confines of his own self-constructed "self."[7] Making himself the sole arbiter of

---

[4] Michael Ffinch, *G. K. Chesterton: A Biography*, San Francisco: Harper & Row, 1986, p. 258

[5] *Homo viator*: an understanding that man's essential purpose is to love and serve God in this world so that he might be with Him eternally in the next. *Homo viator* is man as pilgrim; man as a wayfarer who journeys through life with his final destiny and purpose always in mind.

[6] Since modernism and post-modernism are merely different manifestations of the errors of *homo superbus*, the two terms will be conflated into the word "modern" throughout the remainder of the essay.

[7] *Homo superbus*: an understanding that man's essential purpose is to love and serve himself. He is motivated by the sin of *superbia*, the pride that animated Satan's rebellion, and Adam and Eve's. There is no better presentation of *homo superbus* than the character of Polonius

all "truth" and "morality," he has shrunk the cosmos to the size of his own ego. He is the de facto god of his own creation. He is, in fact, such a pathetic creature that he does not even know that he is a creature, in the sense that he does not know or arrogantly denies that he has been created. And it is this creature, so prevalent and so dominant in the modern academy, that Chesterton seeks to engage and convert throughout the corpus of his work. To put the matter succinctly, Chesterton's engagement with the principles of education is nothing less than the efforts of *homo viator* to make *homo superbus* see the truth beyond himself.

"The one thing that is never taught by any chance in the atmosphere of public schools," wrote Chesterton, "is ... that there is a whole truth of things, and that in knowing it and speaking it we are happy."[8] Such words would be greeted with calculated coldness by the architects of the modern academy, who would no doubt respond with chilling indifference that there is no whole truth of things and therefore no meaningful happiness to be derived from it. Modernity never gets beyond Pontius Pilate's famous question, *quid est veritas*, which is asked not in the spirit of philosophy as a question to be answered, but in the ennui of intellectual philandery as

---

in *Hamlet*, who concludes his disastrous advice to his son with the words, "This above all: To thine own self be true."

[8] G. K. Chesterton, *All Things Considered*, New York: John Lane Company, 1910, p. 153

merely a rhetorical question that is intrinsically unanswerable. This intellectual philandery spawns numerous illegitimate children, each of which has its day as the dominant fad of educationists, at least until a new intellectual fad replaces it. It is in the nature of fads to fade, but in the brief period in which they find themselves in the fashionable limelight they can cause a great deal of damage, a fact that Chesterton addressed with customary adroitness in 1910, over a century ago:

> The trouble in too many of our modern schools is that the State, being controlled so specially by the few, allows cranks[9] and experiments to go straight to the schoolroom when they have never passed through the Parliament, the public house, the private house, the church, or the marketplace.
>
> Obviously it ought to be the oldest things that are taught to the youngest people; the assured and experienced truths that are put first to the baby. But in a school today the baby has to submit to a system that is younger than himself. The flopping infant of four actually has more experience, and has weathered the world longer than the dogma to which he is made to submit.
>
> Many a school boasts of having the last ideas in education, when it has not even the first

---

[9] Chesterton is employing "crank" in its British sense, i.e. a crank as a dangerous eccentric.

idea; for the first idea is that even innocence, divine as it is, may learn something from experience.[10]

Implicit in Chesterton's critique of the nature of modern education is the intellectual elitism that fuels the fads and fashions of the zeitgeist. The antidote to the poison of elitism, in Chesterton's mind, is the populism and common sense of democracy; and the antidote to the transience of intellectual fads and fashions is the timeless touchstone of Tradition. For Chesterton, tradition is the extension of democracy through time, the proxy of the dead and the enfranchisement of the unborn:

> Tradition may be defined as an extension of the franchise. Tradition means giving votes to the most obscure of all classes, our ancestors. It is the democracy of the dead. Tradition refuses to submit to the small and arrogant oligarchy of those who merely happen to be walking about. All democrats object to men being disqualified by the accident of birth; tradition objects to their being disqualified by the accident of death. Democracy tells us not to neglect a good man's opinion, even if he is our groom; tradition asks us not to neglect a good man's opinion, even if he is our father. I,

---

[10] G. K. Chesterton, *What's Wrong with the World*, New York: Dodd, Mead and Company, 1910, p. 255

at any rate, cannot separate the two ideas of democracy and tradition.[11]

It is, of course, obvious that the disenfranchisement of the dead inherent in the modern academy's mania for novelty is also a disenfranchisement of the unborn. In denigrating and deriding the great books of Western civilization, and the great ideas that informed them, the doyens of the modern academy have broken the continuum by which the wisdom of the ages is transmitted to each new generation. In refusing any authority beyond the self, *homo superbus* has disinherited himself; in imposing his egocentric ethos on the academy, he is also disinheriting future generations. Chesterton described modern man as a cad who contemptuously kicks down the ladder by which he's climbed,[12] but the modern academic is even worse. He not only kicks down the ladder by which he's climbed, he tries to destroy the ladder so that no one coming after him can climb it either.

"The purpose of Compulsory Education," wrote Chesterton, "is to deprive the common people of their common sense."[13] This is manifest in the dogmatic imposition of radical relativism, which is the only

---

[11] G. K. Chesterton, *Collected Works, Vol. 1*, San Francisco: Ignatius Press, p. 251

[12] G. K. Chesterton, *The Defendant*, London: R. Brimley Johnson, 1902, p. 6; see also, Chesterton, *A Miscellany of Men*, New York: Dodd, Mead and Company, 1912, p. 305

[13] G. K. Chesterton, *Illustrated London News*, Sep. 7, 1929

philosophy compatible with *homo superbus*, and the implementation of secular fundamentalism, the political ideology of *homo superbus*, an ideology that refuses to tolerate anything but the things it tolerates itself, and does so in the name of "tolerance," an egregious and outrageous example of the sheer chutzpah of Orwellian double-think. In short, *homo superbus* has re-created education in his own image and has sacrificed all rival dogmas on the altar of self-worship that he has erected for himself, on which the tabernacle has been replaced by the mirror of self-referential subjectivism. There is no place in such self-referential education for religion or for any metaphysical philosophy.

The *reductio ad absurdum* at the heart of such a system of education was certainly not lost on Chesterton, who perceived it as the very antithesis of the object of a true education:

> The only real object of all education is to teach people the proportions of things, that they may see what things are large and what small: we seem bent on teaching people to prefer in everything what is small to what is great, what is doubtful to what is certain, and what is trivial to what is eternal.[14]

---

[14] Ibid., Aug. 24, 1912

Chesterton made the same point even more succinctly and sublimely in an epigrammatic turn of phrase that should serve as a motto for all true educators: "The whole point of education is that it should give a man abstract and eternal standards by which he can judge material and fugitive standards."[15] The problem is that radical relativism believes that there are no abstract and eternal standards but that, on the contrary, all standards are merely fugitive, here today and gone tomorrow. Education does not serve Truth because there is no truth to serve. Chesterton's *bon mot* will not serve as a motto for the modern academy because the modern academy does not serve anything but itself. Its motto is *non serviam*. In such circumstances, education ceases to be the means to an end because there is no end, in the objective sense of a purpose or meaning to life. In consequence, the means, having no end, becomes an end in itself. The purpose of education for modern educators is simply education itself. "It is typical of our time," Chesterton wrote, "that the more doubtful we are about the value of philosophy, the more certain we are about the value of education. That is to say, the more doubtful we are about whether we have any truth, the more certain we are (apparently) that we can teach it to children. The smaller our faith in doctrine, the larger our faith in doctors..."[16]

---

[15] Ibid., Sep. 29, 1930
[16] Ibid., Jan. 12, 1907

The absence of theology and philosophy from the core of the modern academy leads inevitably, in Chesterton's view, to two mutually incompatible educational concepts attempting to coexist, and this, in turn, constitutes a schism or schizophrenia at the very heart of the academy itself:

> The truth is that the modern world has committed itself to two totally different and inconsistent conceptions about education. It is always trying to expand the scope of education; and always trying to exclude from it all religion and philosophy. But this is sheer nonsense. You can have an education that teaches atheism because atheism is true, and it can be, from its own point of view, a complete education. But you cannot have an education claiming to teach all truth, and then refusing to discuss whether atheism is true.[17]

The absurdity of the modern academy's attempt to build a university in the absence of universals was a topic to which Chesterton would return often. "Take away the supernatural," says Chesterton, "and what remains is the unnatural."[18] "Education is only the truth in a state of

---

[17] G. K. Chesterton, *The Common Man*, New York: Sheed & Ward, 1950, p. 168-9
[18] G. K. Chesterton, *Collected Works, Vol. 1*, p. 88

transmission," he wrote on another occasion, "and how can we pass on truth if it has never come into our hand?"[19]

One consequence of this lack of truthfulness in the academy was what Chesterton called "standardization by a low standard,"[20] a dumbing-down of standards to a lowest common denominator of prescribed mediocrity. In the absence of an integrated curriculum in which each discipline informs the other, each part making sense in the light of the whole, the modern academy has literally disintegrated itself into a plethora of fragmented particles, none of which is in communication with the other parts. "Everything has been sundered from everything else, and everything has grown cold. Soon we shall hear of specialists dividing the tune from the words of a song, on the ground that they spoil each other ... This world is all one wild divorce court."[21]

Ironically, in exorcising the unifying spirit of theology and philosophy from the core curriculum, the modern academy doomed itself to fractious fragmentation, in which each discipline exiled itself from all the others. In excommunicating theology and philosophy, the modern academy has paradoxically excommunicated itself from itself! "Because the

---

[19] G. K. Chesterton, *What's Wrong with the World*, pp. 192-3
[20] G. K. Chesterton, *Culture and the Coming Peril*, being the text of a speech delivered by Chesterton at the University of London in 1928; reprinted in the *Chesterton Review*, Vol. 18, No. 2, August 1992
[21] G. K. Chesterton, *What's Wrong with the World*, p. 152

elementary school doesn't teach theology," wrote Chesterton, "it must be excused when it doesn't teach anything. The bias of the modern world is so enormous that it will allow a thing to be inefficient as long as it is also irreligious."[22] The anti-religious spirit of modernity is so antagonistic to the idea of a unifying truth that it prefers a meaningless education to an education informed by the underlying meaning inherent in the truth claims of religion or philosophy. And this, according to Chesterton, is not really education at all: "Every education teaches a philosophy; if not by dogma then by suggestion, by implication, by atmosphere. Every part of that education has a connection with every other part. If it does not all combine to convey some general view of life, it is not an education at all."[23] This integrated view of a liberal arts education is contrasted with the disintegrated education of the relativist: "There is something to be said for teaching everything to somebody, as compared with the modern notion of teaching nothing, and the same sort of nothing, to everybody."[24] Whereas the former conveys a philosophy by which one can understand the cosmos, the latter "is not a philosophy but the art of reading and writing

---

[22] G. K. Chesterton, *Illustrated London News*, July 18, 1914
[23] G. K. Chesterton, *The Common Man*, p. 166
[24] G. K. Chesterton, *All I Survey*, London: Methuen, 1933, p. 50

unphilosophically."[25] The former teaches its recipient how to think; the latter prevents its victim from thinking.

This absence of thought and the ability to think is the tragedy of modern education because we cannot understand the other subjects on the curriculum if we cannot understand philosophy and theology. Take the study of history, for instance. If historians have never been taught philosophy and theology they have been excommunicated from the past. They do not understand who makes history, what makes history, and why history is made. They do not *understand*. Once again, Chesterton diagnoses the problem with unfailing precision:

> About half the history now taught in schools and colleges is made windy and barren by the narrow notion of leaving out the theological theories ... Historians seem to have completely forgotten two facts—first, that men act from ideas; and second, that it might, therefore, be as well to discover which ideas.[26]

Properly understood, history is a chronological map that shows us not only where we have come from but also where we are, and how we got here. It is also possible to project where we are likely to be going in the future by drawing the line of knowledge on the chronological map

[25] Ibid.
[26] G. K. Chesterton, *Illustrated London News*, May 13, 1911

from where we have come from to where we are now, and extending the line into the realm of future possibilities. In this sense history can also be a prophet. It increases our knowledge of the past, present, and future. This, however, is only true if the chronological map is accurate. If it has been drawn by those with prejudiced perceptions or a prejudiced agenda, it will only succeed in getting us lost. There are few things more dangerous than an inaccurate map, especially if we find ourselves in perilous terrain.

In the context of the study of history, the objective truth requires the knowledge of three distinct facets of historical reality, namely historical *chronology*, historical *mechanics*, and historical *philosophy*, i.e., *when* things happened, *how* things happened and *why* things happened. The last of these, though it is dependent factually on the other two, is the most important. If we don't know why things happened, history remains devoid of meaning; it makes no sense. As such, historians must have knowledge of the history of belief. They must know *what* people believed *when* they did the things that they did in order to know *why* they acted as they did. They must have empathy with the great ideas that shaped human history, even if they don't have sympathy with them. This whole issue was addressed with great lucidity by Chesterton's great friend, Hilaire Belloc, perhaps the most important historian of the twentieth century (with the possible exception of Christopher Dawson):

The worst fault in [writing] history ... is the fault of not knowing what the spiritual state of those whom one describes really was. Gibbon and his master Voltaire, the very best of reading, are for that reason bad writers of history. To pass through the tremendous history of the Trinitarian dispute from which our civilization arose and to treat it as a farce is not history. To write the story of the sixteenth century in England and to make of either the Protestant or the Catholic a grotesque is to miss history altogether.[27]

Clearly frustrated at the supercilious approach towards the past that blinded many historians, Belloc offers a practical example of its effects upon scholarship:

There is an enormous book called Volume 1 of a *Cambridge History of the Middle Ages*. It is 759 pages in length of close print ... It does not mention the Mass once. That is as though you were to write a history of the Jewish dispersion without mentioning the synagogue or of the

[27] Hilaire Belloc, *A Conversation with an Angel and Other Essays*, London: Jonathan Cape, 1928, pp. 166-7

British Empire without mentioning the City of London or the Navy ...[28]

In order to avoid the chronological snobbery that presumes the superiority of the present over the past and which causes this lack of proportion and focus, historians must see history through the eyes of the past, not the present. They must put themselves into the minds and hearts of the protagonists they are studying; and to do this adequately they must have knowledge of philosophy and theology in order to *understand* their own academic discipline and in order to remain disciplined in their study of it. An ignorance of philosophy and theology means an ignorance of history.

For Belloc and Chesterton, therefore, history is best studied through the prism of theology, a fact that has effectively made the study of history impossible in the post-theological modern academy. And what is true of history is equally true of literature. The modern academy fails to see that an ignorance of theology and philosophy disqualifies most literature professors from being able to understand the literature that they purport to teach. Meanwhile art historians claim to be able to "explain" the meaning of medieval and Renaissance paintings without a knowledge of the philosophy and theology that was their inspiration and their purpose. And so we see how

---

[28] Robert Speaight (ed.), *Letters from Hilaire Belloc*, London: Hollis & Carter, 1958, p. 75

the tragedy of modern education metamorphoses into a comedy of errors.

Before we return to Chesterton, it is worth noting, in passing, that Chesterton's critique of the follies and fallacies at the heart of the modern academy has been echoed by the generation of great writers who followed in his wake. T. S. Eliot's *Modern Education and the Classics*, published in 1934, complemented C. S. Lewis's own "Reflections on Education with Special Reference to the Teaching of English," which was the subtitle of his book, *The Abolition of Man*. Both works insisted that education could not be divorced from morality and that the latter must inform the former. Similarly, Eliot's *The Idea of a Christian Society* (1939) and his *Notes Towards the Definition of Culture* (1948) dovetailed with Lewis's position as regards the necessity of Christianity to any genuine restoration of European culture. Most notably, Eliot's depiction of "The Hollow Men" in his poem of that title, published in 1925, prefigures Lewis's "Men without Chests" in *The Abolition of Man* who are fictionalized to great satirical effect in Lewis's *That Hideous Strength*, the latter of which contains a delightful parody of the disintegration and dumbing-down of the modern academy.

Evelyn Waugh, in his magnum opus, *Brideshead Revisited*, a novel which was itself inspired by a line in one of Chesterton's *Father Brown* stories, lampoons the "hollow men" produced by the modern academy in his portrayal of Hooper and Rex Mottram. Hooper had "no special illusions distinguishable from the general, enveloping fog from which he observed the universe":

Hooper had wept often, but never for Henry's speech on St. Crispin's day, nor for the epitaph at Thermopylae. The history they taught him had had few battles in it but, instead, a profusion of detail about humane legislation and recent industrial change. Gallipoli, Balaclava, Quebec, Lepanto, Bannockburn, Roncesvales, and Marathon – these, and the Battle in the West where Arthur fell, and a hundred such names whose trumpet-notes, even now in my sere and lawless state, called to me irresistibly across the intervening years with all the clarity and strength of boyhood, sounded in vain to Hooper ...

In the weeks that we were together Hooper became a symbol to me of Young England, so that whenever I read some public utterance proclaiming what Youth demanded in the Future and what the world owed to Youth, I would test these general statements by substituting 'Hooper' and seeing if they still seemed as plausible. Thus in the dark hour before reveille I sometimes pondered: 'Hooper Rallies', 'Hooper Hostels', 'International Hooper

Cooperation', and 'the Religion of Hooper'. He was the acid test of all these alloys.[29]

Like Hooper, the character of Rex Mottram serves as a personification of the product of the modern, disintegrated academy. In the words of Julia, he illustrates not only the ignorance of those who have been afflicted by the inadequacies of modern education, but the ignorance of their ignorance that is the hallmark of the "hollow man" or the *homo superbus*:

> You know Father Mowbray hit on the truth about Rex at once, that it took me a year of marriage to see. He simply wasn't all there. He wasn't a complete human being at all. He was a tiny bit of one, unnaturally developed ... I thought the was a sort of primitive savage, but he was something absolutely modern and up-to-date that only this ghastly age could produce. A tiny bit of a man pretending he was whole ...[30]

Returning to Chesterton, it seems decorous that we should conclude in a manner that does justice to the great man's wit as well as his wisdom. In Chesterton's handwritten ripostes to the epigrams in Holbrook

---

[29] Evelyn Waugh, *Brideshead Revisited*, New York: Alfred A. Knopf, Everyman's Library, 1993, pp. 8-9
[30] Ibid., pp. 181-2

Jackson's *Platitudes in the Making*, published in 1911, we see a timeless exchange between the radical relativism of the zeitgeist and the Christian realism of the everlasting man. We also see how easily *homo viator* vanquishes *homo superbus* in a fair fight:

Jackson: Be contented, when you have got all you want.
Chesterton: Till then, be happy.
Jackson: Don't think – do.
Chesterton: Do think! Do!
Jackson: A lie is that which you do not believe.
Chesterton: This is a lie: so perhaps you don't believe it.
Jackson: As soon as an idea is accepted it is time to reject it.
Chesterton: No: it is time to build another idea on it. You are always rejecting: and you build nothing.
Jackson: Truth and falsehood in the abstract do not exist.
Chesterton: Then nothing else does.
Jackson: Truth is one's own conception of things.
Chesterton: The Big Blunder. All thought is an attempt to discover if one's own conception is true or not.
Jackson: No two men have exactly the same religion: a church, like society, is a compromise.
Chesterton: The same religion has the two men. The sun shines on the Evil and the Good. But the sun does not compromise.
Jackson: Only the rich preach content to the poor.
Chesterton: When they are not preaching Socialism.

Jackson: In a beautiful city an art gallery would be superfluous. In an ugly one it is a narcotic.

Chesterton: In a real one it is an art gallery.

Jackson: Negations without affirmations are worthless.

Chesterton: And impossible.

Jackson: Theology and religion are not the same thing. When the churches are controlled by the theologians religious people stay away.

Chesterton: Theology is simply that part of religion that requires brains.

Jackson: Desire to please God is never disinterested.

Chesterton: Well, I should hope not!

Jackson: We are more inclined to regret our virtues than our vices; but only the very honest will admit this.

Chesterton: I don't regret any virtues except those I have lost.

Jackson: Every custom was once an eccentricity; every idea was once an absurdity.

Chesterton: No, no, no. Some ideas were always absurdities. This is one of them.

Jackson: No opinion matters finally: except your own.

Chesterton: Said the man who thought he was a rabbit.[31]

On pondering the sheer inanity of Jackson's "platitudes" one is reminded insistently of another Chestertonian witticism, expressed in his regular newspaper column

---

[31] Quoted in Joseph Pearce, *Wisdom and Innocence: A Life of G.K. Chesterton*, San Francisco: Ignatius Press, 1996, pp. 172-3

many years later: "To say that the moderns are half-educated may seem to be too complimentary by half."[32]

Witticisms aside, the great tragedy, and greater comedy, of *homo superbus* is that he doesn't exist. He is a figment of his own imagination. He is, whether he knows it or not or likes it or not, exactly like the rest of us. He is *homo viator*. If, however, he insists on believing he is something that he is not, there is little we can do for him. He must be left to his fantasies, obliviously ignorant of his ignorance. And although he is lost—and there are none so lost as those who do not know that they are lost—there is no reason for future generations to follow him into the wilderness. The task for those of us who have not succumbed to the malaise of modern education is to ensure that future generations have the gift of a real and true education. As Chesterton said, and it is right that the last word is his: "Teach, to the young, men's enduring truths, and let the learned amuse themselves with their passing errors."[33]

---

[32] G. K. Chesterton, *Illustrated London News*, June 2, 1928
[33] G. K. Chesterton, *Illustrated London News*, Oct 15, 1910

3

Where Wonder Leads
Ruth Popp[34]

Ruth Popp earned her Bachelor of Science from the United States Naval Academy in1989. Over the past 18 years she has been homeschooling one or more of her 5 daughters. Personal growth as an educator led Ruth to admiration for and ultimately enthusiastic engagement in the classical education renewal gaining strength across the nation. She currently serves as Director and President of the Board for St. Thomas Aquinas Tutorial in Arnold, MD, and Vice President of Classic Learning Initiatives.

---

[34] This essay was originally published on 16 September 2016 at www.CirceInstitute.org under the title "Where Wonder Led Me."

We didn't know wonder was enlivening our home until it died. My oldest daughter Frances, so full of questions and curiosity, had ensured that we saw the world with fresh eyes and contagious awe. But after a military move across the country in the middle of her kindergarten year, we settled into base housing. The principal of the local Title I public school stated firmly that her goal was to break the cycle of poverty for some children and therefore she would not assign her best teachers or resources to "smart kids from intact families." So we chose a local private school and then watched in horror as our vivacious thirsty learner stopped asking questions, stopped wondering about the world, and began focusing on Beanie Baby labels and social status.

Increasingly, she regarded me less as a mother than a chauffeur. The only thing I knew about education was that it was not happening, though I could not articulate or understand the problem. This early crisis awoke a million questions in me. What is education? How do you know if your child is getting a good one? What is the goal? Does it matter how you get there? My questions led me to consider every option, including the ridiculous notion of home education. My early inquiries into the world of homeschooling proceeded with a particular prayer running through my mind, "Please God, don't ask me to do this." And then the lights came on.

What began as dread at the very thought of myself as a teacher morphed quickly into the planning stage of a great adventure. Soon I rediscovered my own love for books, bugs, and beauty. And I thrilled to see curiosity and awe stir in my sweet daughter's gaze. One month into first grade, in the middle of our read-aloud, I caught her looking at me with awe and amazement. I paused to hear what had inspired her reverence. With luminous eyes she declared, "Mom, you can read really well!" In that moment, she moved me beyond "chauffeur status" and opened her mind and heart to whatever lessons I chose to teach. This journey was restoring not only her intellect, but our relationship as well. I began to understand that a good education concerns itself with right relationships: with God, self, others, the natural world, etc. During those first years of rapid discovery, I wandered to a ledge with a breathtaking view: the idea of classical education.

Classical education became my next frontier. I would wander this land of opportunity for years before I began to recognize its geographical features, its weather patterns, and its deep waters. What do I love the most about it? It is real and satisfying. It is worthy of my trust, for it has been tested by millennia rather than one or two generations of devoted fans. The particular enduring stories, the Great Books and the good books which train us for their coming, speak across the ages sharing the truth about ourselves and our journey in a way that requires us to climb, harvest, peel, and taste the truth which has the power to set us free should we choose to consume it. I am a newcomer to this province, with most of the land untouched before me. Still, here I am in my nineteenth year of homeschooling, and my ninth year attempting to educate classically. Predictably, this wonder led me to share my joy by collaborating in founding and leading a classical tutorial for homeschoolers. However, wonder has a way of calling us to the unexpected as well. I am now close to the end of my homeschooling season. Many changes have altered the educational landscape. I have seen three daughters through the college application process, and I have begun to appreciate the life cycle of pre-college education in the United States. What begins in wonder with a focus on goodness and good citizenship in kindergarten, ends with standardized college entrance exams whose selected texts would lead us to believe that we cannot know what is good, and that truth does not exist. Once students have accepted the idea that truth does not exist, they have been crippled in their ability to recognize and respond to the One who is Truth. The dawning of this provocative realization caused me to wonder about the nature and impact of standardized college entrance exams upon the entire educational system.

These high-stakes tests do more than measure. They drive curricula down into high schools, middle schools, and grammar schools. In steering curricula, they drastically alter what is taught. For example, AP U.S History courses across the nation were significantly rewritten over the summer of 2014 to align with the politically correct agenda of the new AP U.S. History exam. Test writers controlled what the most able history students of this nation would know of their own cultural inheritance. The tests are more powerful than I had imagined. The two college entrance testing behemoths—in abandoning any claim to ethics, goodness, and truth—have emptied our educational systems of teaching that might endow students with a working moral compass.

I arrived more slowly to this horrific understanding than other education minded peers. My friend Amy, in lamenting the situation, asked me, "Are all these colleges and educational associations who profess allegiance to true liberal arts education going to continue measuring our children by these degraded and degrading standardized tests?" I thought, "Yes, what are they going to do? Who will stop talking and start acting?" Shortly thereafter, Jeremy Tate, of Classic Learning Initiatives, invited me to work with his team in the audacious task of bringing a new standardized college entrance exam into being. I began to wonder anew. Can this be done? Could *we* do this? The great stories have taught me that those who stand against giants are not often wise by human standards, nor powerful, nor of noble birth. By these benchmarks, I find myself qualified to join the movement. Wonder has led me to my next great adventure: the Classic Learning Test.

The Classic Learning Test (CLT) invites students to wrestle with works of the greatest minds in the history of the Western tradition across literary and mathematical content. Rich material reflecting both theistic and secular perspectives challenges students to analyze and comprehend texts that are not just concerned with one small, narrow topic but rather represent the scope and complexity of life, including the moral implications and the far reaching consequences of ideas, passions, action, inaction, scientific inquiry, and love.

In joining the CLT team, I find myself, once again, standing at a new frontier with much to learn. A million fresh questions are born. Beautiful views appear as I discover brilliant initiatives gaining traction in American education. They begin with one or two people beholding great need, wondering at potential solutions, and setting to work.

And now, I have to ask: Where is wonder leading you?

4

Happiness and the Moral Dimension of Education

Michael Bors

Michael Bors, a native of Annapolis, Maryland, is a doctoral student in the School of Philosophy at Catholic University of America. He is currently writing a thesis on Boethius, Aquinas, and the forms of false happiness. Michael graduated from Thomas Aquinas College in 2015 with a double major in philosophy and theology, having defended a thesis on the philosophical and empirical methods of studying the natural world. Michael also studied classics, economics, and music at George Mason University, and Latin, French, and Spanish at several other institutions.

A city can be virtuous only when the citizens who have a share in the government are virtuous, and in our state all the citizens share in the government; let us then inquire how a man becomes virtuous. (Aristotle, *Politics*)

We maintain, and have said in the Ethics, if the arguments there adduced are of any value, that happiness is the realization and perfect exercise of virtue, and this not conditional, but absolute. (Aristotle, *Politics*)

What view presents itself as we look out today across the landscape of American education? One feature is clear: a new path from grade school to college has been laid, bypassing terrain that was once central to the educational journey. While students used to cover such ground as the Greek and Roman classics, English literature, and moral philosophy, these subjects today are considered only in passing. Along with this, the ethical dimension of education is largely neglected. The great questions about character and moral virtue which are so central to human life are often deemed too controversial to consider in the classroom.

The older educational path, however, has not been completely abandoned. In fact, many students, parents, and teachers, skeptical of the "value-neutral" method, are returning to a more traditional education, meant for the whole person. In these schools, students are exploring the richness of the Western tradition, and reading about and discussing the ethical dimensions of life. In recent years, many associations and schools have been formed to promote such education. The growing popularity of homeschooling, charter schools, and religious secondary schools is promising, as is the work of many smaller liberal arts and religious schools. There are reasons for hope too in the mainstream academy, where honors colleges, core studies, and great books seminars provide space for this kind of education.

This essay explores the underlying principles behind this movement toward humane and ethical education. The connection between intellectual pursuit and virtue was well understood by the ancients; we will therefore draw on their wisdom for this discussion. In the first part of the essay, we will consider generally the nature of virtue, and its connection to living a happy life. In the second, we will explore how, far from being easy or automatic, virtue requires careful attention and training. In the third part, we will show how virtue accordingly requires not only a moral upbringing by parents and religious communities, but formal education in ethics and the virtues. In the conclusion, we will show how these themes connect to the mission of the Classic Learning Test.

Part I: Virtue and Happiness

What do we mean by "virtue," in the first place? While the word in general conversation today can sometimes sound stuffy or old-fashioned, both the Latin word from which "virtue" derives and its Greek equivalent carry the sense of "valor," "bravery," and more generally, "moral excellence." Therefore there is something splendid about a virtuous person, a vitality which shines out from his character. As Socrates describes in the *Republic*: "Virtue, then, as it seems, would be a certain health, beauty and good condition of a soul, and vice a sickness, ugliness and weakness." Now just as health implies a right proportion between the several parts of the body, so virtue implies a proper order between the several "parts" of the soul. Since the soul's powers include emotions, appetites, will, and mind, whoever possesses virtue enjoys a harmonious activity of these, all cooperating for the good of the whole person. Furthermore, virtue is habitual. More than a single good choice, virtue is a long-lasting disposition to right feeling and action.

What then does virtue have to do with real human life? According to the greatest philosophers of the Western tradition and others, virtue is the only way to a happy and fulfilling life. Living well means living according to the intellectual and moral virtues. The truth of this claim appears in our daily human experience. While many set their sights on securing wealth, reputation, beauty, and so on, it is the intellectually and morally virtuous who most closely achieve happiness. When someone older, a trusted figure in the school or community, passes on some wisdom he or she has stored up over a lifetime, the desirability of understanding is clear. Likewise, great acts of virtue by heroes or saints impress all of us, because we see that, in some way, that is what a human being is meant to be. As Aristotle explains: "Happiness ... is found in larger measure with those who are of surpassingly high cultivation in character and intellect but only moderate as regards the external acquisition of goods."

At the end of the fourth book of the *Republic*, Socrates has discovered a meaning of justice, which we might take more generally as the interior condition of the virtuous soul. The person who has justice "really sets his own house in good order and rules himself; he arranges himself, becomes his own friend, and harmonizes the three parts [of the soul] ... [He] becomes entirely one from many, moderate and harmonized. Then, and only then, he acts ... " The life such a person experiences stands far above the turbulence of the wildly passionate person. With the right character, living a satisfying and fulfilling life becomes possible.

Part II: The Road to Virtue
Granting the supreme value of virtue, we next come to the question, "How does a person become virtuous?" As Aristotle explains, "there are three things by which people

become good and virtuous. These three are nature, habit, and reason." We will consider each of these in turn. Taking the first, nature, we recognize that we are human beings, which is to say animals enlivened by a rational soul, physical beings sparked with the divine, persons made in the image of God. We owe such great thanks for having been gifted with such a nature. What possibilities it entails, what heights it promises, but what responsibilities it demands! In order to become fully human, then, we must live in accordance with this dual nature. Our happiness thus will coincide with the good functioning of body and soul. Furthermore, if education means to "lead us out" of obscurity and confusion, then it must do so by illuminating the understanding and shaping the character.

The second thing which assists virtue is habit. Now habit is formed as the result of repeated activity in one strain or another; we are what we repeatedly do. Just as a dancer can perform her dance only after repeated practice of those beautiful motions, so a person can act prudently only through repeated acts of choosing well. In both cases what is done regularly becomes custom, and custom becomes a "second nature," guiding a person down certain well-trodden paths. Habits, however, begin to develop long before a child becomes conscious of choosing what is good for its own sake; therefore the task of shaping these habits first falls to parents. Thus acquiring mature virtue is nearly impossible when one lacks the early moral formation which parents supply, as Aristotle points out: "It makes no small difference, then, whether one is habituated in this or that way straight from childhood but a very great difference—or rather the whole difference."

Consider too how the Athenian speaks in Plato's *Laws*: "Now I mean by education that training which is given by suitable habits to the first instincts of virtue in children—when pleasure, and friendship, and pain, and hatred, are rightly implanted in souls not yet capable of understanding the nature of them, and who find them, after they have attained reason, to be in harmony with her." Thus education begins in a household in which children are brought up well. The habits generated and nourished in the home will be the supports of good study in school, and the foundation of a strong ethical character.

We now turn to reason, the third and greatest of the things "by which men become good and virtuous." Human rationality sits at the peak of what it means to be human, and just as the summit is the last place reached in a hike, so in the progress of education, rationality in its fullness comes only after much preparation. It is a characteristic of reason that through it a man is conscious and aware of what is good. While a child might say "please" and "thank you" as a result of habitual encouragement, someone more mature does so with a consciousness of the ease and mutual respect that good manners promote. The rational moral agent does not stand haughtily above habits, but rather he raises them to their most complete level by connecting them with a conscious, rational choice for the good.

Part III: Virtue and Formal Education
Why is education necessary for the development of virtue? It is necessary because *reason* can best be nourished and fed by means of formal study. In academic classes, whether they take place at an institution or a homeschool, serious and sustained attention can be devoted to study at a higher level than is possible in the regular course of daily life. Teachers can engage each part of the student's soul. Stories, poems, and literature fill the imagination with pictures of good and evil, in which what is admirable shines out, filling the heart with the desire for imitation. History feeds the memory with great examples of men and women of the past who served God or their country in great ways. History also tells of wicked men, so that students can appreciate what decent people must beware of and fight against. Even the senses can partake in this formation of character, insofar as the fine arts imitate the passion and types of character. Through beautiful music the soul experiences certain feelings, which can become habitual. Similarly, a statue or painting of a great statesman reveals something of his character, instructing those who see it.

Finally and most importantly, the student's mind itself should be fed with instruction of moral duties, obligations, and of the good as such, so that what has been repeatedly grasped at other levels can now be rationally affirmed. For example, the stories of good and evil we have heard from childhood are not just quaint tales, but manifestations of what is true, good, and beautiful. While the child "feels" this at a basic level, the educated person is able to know the deeper moral causes. All of these dimensions of education help the student grow into a mature love for wisdom and goodness.

Now, it would be too simplistic to say that a good curriculum simply makes students good. Even if teachers assign authors who write about morals, and explore with their students the duties and responsibilities of virtuous members of society, this does not guarantee that all students will become outstanding individuals. What is certain, however, is that the ideal matters. An educational system in which virtue is honored and held up as an ideal, and in which teachers and students come to respect and love it as something intensely desirable, will do more good for the students and the community at large than a school system in which virtue is belittled as relative, brushed aside as trivial, or flat-out ignored. Even though we men and women fall far short of our aims, we must recognize the precious value of what we strive for.

Other purposes have been offered to explain education. One common understanding measures an education by how well it moves a student into a "good" school, which will be a stepping stone for a "successful" career, *i.e.*, one that is financially rewarding. Now no one can deny that a gratifying career and comfortable lifestyle are desirable things. The point, however, is that there is another, more essential purpose for education: to cultivate the intellectual and moral virtues, that is, to help make students wise and good. Without these qualities, wealth cannot even be put to good use.

At this point, some might push back against the assertion that schools should concern themselves with the ethical formation of their students. For is not the family charged with bringing up children according to moral standards, and should not the church or religious community provide them with the broader principles and context of moral life? Some might consider school-based ethical education as an intrusion into the sanctuary of the family and its responsibilities and privileges. What is more, it sometimes seems the "values" which educators would try to impose on students are contrary to the very standards parents work so hard to instill.

The answer to this objection, of course, is that families, schools, and churches all must cooperate in the education of the child. The family is indeed the primary place in which children are brought up into a moral and ethical life, first through habituation, and later through explicit teaching. Again, the church or religious community is essential to connecting this familial instruction with the larger society, and connecting our society in a public way with a higher spiritual life. Yet these truths do not conflict with our claim that the school must play an important part in the ethical formation of the student. These three institutions complement and support one another in the task of intellectual and moral education. In the right order of things, the school teachers receive from parents ethically well-disposed students, and provide them with formal education in ethics, literature, history, and other areas. by which they become educated and mature human beings. Schools must provide the rich intellectual and cultural soil in which children's moral roots can grow stronger and deeper.

Conclusion: The Role of the CLT

To review the principles we have explored: our common human nature endows us with a body, emotions, desires, will, and a mind. A satisfying and happy life can only exist when these various parts are in harmony, working together for the true good of the whole person and his community. Virtue therefore stands as the preeminent moral good. Acquiring it, however, is difficult, and requires much work by many people over a long period of time. One of the essential stages in the moral development of the person comes with formal education. School teachers can and must guide their students to a higher awareness and appreciation for the moral good, and they can do this by presenting philosophical texts and poetic and literary works which concern moral teaching and ethical inquiry. The Classic Learning Test provides colleges with a truly holistic standard for evaluating applicants. While other standardized tests seek to measure academic potential in a "value-neutral" way, the CLT presents challenging and important ethical texts from the Western tradition and asks the students to grapple with their meaning. The test does not neglect the traditional academic evaluations of verbal reasoning, grammatical and writing ability, and mathematical skill – these are evaluated just as with the other tests. The CLT, however, integrates them into the larger project of holistic and liberal education. The test thus provides a standard for those who, avoiding the value-free path to education, have returned to the more traditional path of education. It is an affirmative measure for parents, students, teachers, and college admissions staff who care about the union of intellectual pursuit and virtue and wish to see them increase and flourish together.

Part II

Questioning the Standard

5

No Neutrality:
The Myth of Objective Standardized University Admissions Tests
Roy Alden Atwood

Roy Alden Atwood (Ph.D., Iowa) is the Deputy Head of Nehemiah Gateway University in Buçimas, Pogradec, Albania, in southern Europe. He previously served as academic dean and president of New Saint Andrews College, Moscow, Idaho (2000-2015), and is a former professor, administrator, and vice-chair of the faculty at the University of Idaho, Moscow, Idaho (1984-2000). He has twice been a Senior Fulbright Scholar, to Warsaw University in Poland, and to Potchefstroom (now North West) University in South Africa. He was also twice elected an accreditation commissioner by the institutional members of the Transnational Association of Christian Colleges and Schools (tracs.org), a post-secondary accrediting body recognized by the U.S. Department of Education and the Council for Higher Education Accreditation (2010-2015).

> The only objective part of most standardized tests is scoring, when done by an accurately programmed machine. Deciding what items to include on the test, how questions are worded, which answers are scored as 'correct,' how the test is administered, and the uses of exam results are all made by subjective human beings.[35]

The objectivity of standardized college admissions tests is a myth. It remains a persistent and popular myth despite its lack of empirical and theoretical support. The dominant SAT and ACT exams not only fail to achieve what they, and the institutions that require them, claim they achieve, according to a sizable body of critical research, but they do so by standing on a host of questionable assumptions about scientific objectivity and value-neutrality. The objectivity myth enveloping the academic testing industry is disingenuously sustained or quietly acknowledged by the test makers themselves, government agencies, rankings services, and universities. This myth is then peddled to unsuspecting test-takers. There is no objectivity; there is no neutrality. The myth of objectivity is misleading and ultimately

---

[35] Fairtest.org, "What's Wrong With Standardized Tests?" Fairtest.Org website, May 22, 2012; http://fairtest.org/facts/whatwron.htm; accessed Aug. 22, 2016

counterproductive to academic improvement, distortive of college rankings, and overemphasized in admissions decisions. It is this myth of objectivity that nevertheless drives educational policies across the country and sustains a "non-profit" testing industry now worth several billions of dollars. That should change.

The Reification of "Intelligence" and Myth Making
From their heady, early days, standardized test developers, who emerged from trendy new fields such as psychometrics, educational testing, and statistics, justified the making and use of their new tests as a "scientific" and "objective" enterprise for evaluating the knowledge (learning previously acquired) and aptitude (potential for learning) of secondary students. Those early tests (the SAT—initially called the Scholastic *Aptitude* Test—launched in 1926) boasted their "scientific" credentials and methods. The invocation of the terms "science," "scientific methods," and "objectivity" provided enough rhetorical power to impress the less critically minded. Wearing the mantle of "science" was enough to reassure a pliable public of the tests' integrity, trustworthiness, and acceptance. If the tests were presumably written by "scientists," who would seriously question, let alone challenge, the expertise behind such precise measuring instruments? Few did until the 1980s.

The late evolutionary biologist Stephen Jay Gould, in his award-winning book exposing the fallacies behind intelligence (IQ) testing, *The Mismeasure of Man* (1981), criticized "the myth that science itself is an objective enterprise, done properly only when scientists can shuck the constraints of their culture and view the world as it really is." Gould belabored the obvious—that "science must be understood as a social phenomenon, a gutsy, human enterprise, not the work of robots programmed to collect pure information. ... Science, since people must do it, is a socially embedded activity"—because the obvious seemed incapable of countering the power of *the myth* of objective science. For Gould, that myth was embraced and sustained by a naïve public yearning for certitude in an age of ever-shifting uncertainties and by the science community itself, enjoying the trust and confidence placed in it by its fideistic (and remarkably unscientific-minded) fans on Main Street, Wall Street, and Pennsylvania Avenue. But Gould placed the burden of responsibility for this mythic muddle squarely on the shoulders of his scientific colleagues, who should have known better. He further noted that the problem would not go away "until scientists give up the twin myths of objectivity and the inexorable march toward truth." Then echoing the prophetic words of Jesus, Gould insisted that "One must, indeed, locate the beam in one's own eye before interpreting correctly the pervasive motes in everybody else's."[36]

---

[36] Gould, S. *The Mismeasure of Man*. New York: W.W. Norton, 1981, 1996.

Gould astutely observed that early intelligence (IQ) testing, the precursor to today's aptitude and college admission tests, stood on two false, beam-sized assumptions. First was the "reification" of intelligence. Reification or "thing-ifying" is a rhetorical move which turns an abstract concept, process, or set of complex concepts or processes into a single *object* simply by naming it so. A neat trick, if you can pull it off. But just a quick peek behind the wizard's curtain and the initial shock and awe quickly dissipates. The very idea of "science" itself has been reified by a few "true believers" who dearly wish the scientific community would agree more (especially with them and their pet theories), and speak with one, strong, authoritative voice on all matters related to human existence. They are the ones generally prone to declaring, "Science says" or "according to Science." But "science" has no mouth, no voice, no pen. And it shouldn't be capitalized except at the start of a sentence. Particular individuals or teams of scientists speak or write. "Science" does not. Nor does it speak with one voice. Scientists disagree with one another on many things and regularly pursue conflicting methodologies and theories. They often reach different conclusions. So when "Science" is invoked in an honorific and anthropomorphized way, it becomes a reified, special pleading figment of someone's overactive imagination.

This reification of "science" also happened to "intelligence," Gould argues. "This wondrously complex and multifaceted set of human capabilities" that we typically associate with mental activity, thoughtful reflection, imaginative creativity, practical skillfulness, and general wisdom, was reified, turned into a single "thing" called "intelligence" in the early 20th century. Once that trick had been performed, social scientists rushed in to describe it, weigh it, measure it, rank it, and probe it with the most creative empirical methodologies legally allowed. The intelligence/knowledge testing industry was born, and with it quickly followed all the federal research grants Congress could fund.

A second false assumption Gould identified was that, once complex characteristics spanning complex variations in complex conditions were reified into a single object like "intelligence," that entity almost begged to be *ranked* on a gradually ascending scale. Once a person's "intelligence" or "aptitude" or "knowledge" can be reduced to a single number, then one quickly wonders how that number stacks up against other people's numbers. University admissions officers couldn't wait to see who climbed to the top of the food chain. As Gould observed, "[R]anking requires a criterion for assigning all individuals to their proper status in a single series. And what better criterion than an objective number? The common style embodying both fallacies of thought has been quantification, or the measurement of intelligence as a single number for each person."[37] This almost mystical use of numbers, the quantification and ranking of almost everything, may promise a patina of objectivity, a hope for bias-free certitude, but numbers mean nothing by themselves. Without words, we cannot interpret them, explain them, or apply them. Moreover, numbers can be used to lie as much as words. Hence the famous caution (probably first uttered, though variously attributed to Mark Twain and Benjamin Disraeli) by Arthur James Balfour, First Earl of Balfour, "There are three kinds of falsehoods: lies, damned lies, and statistics."

Research Subjects Who Bite Back
One of the key moments in the history of science that helped expose the fallacy of objectivity was Werner Heisenberg's research that led to his "principle of uncertainty." Heisenberg, a theoretical physicist and 1932 winner of the Nobel Prize for the development of quantum mechanics, discovered that one cannot measure or observe *anything* without those acts affecting or influencing the thing being studied in some way. Measuring or observing something affects it simply by its being measured or observed. Heisenberg's research was in the natural sciences. But if a *natural scientist* cannot put something passive and inanimate under a microscope or test it in a lab without affecting it (sometimes seriously

---

[37] Ibid.

so) by the researcher's own body heat, the room's lights, the test tube's surface, the size limits of the petri dish—in fact, all the myriad conditions and contexts in which a researcher places an object to be examined—then *how* much more intrusive is a *social scientist* who tests non-passive, sentient persons, who can look back and even push back? Precisely because they are not passive objects, human respondents to social research can give answers they think the researcher wants to hear or they can lie out of fear or embarrassment in revealing their true answer. If *passive* objects are affected by the research process itself, as Heisenberg discovered, then how much more are the *active* human agents of social research—*people*—affected?

A graduate school friend of mine actually turned the tables on standardized tests in this regard; they became *the objects of his research*. He had no interest in the tests as measures of his intelligence or as predictors of his abilities to perform at the university level. Rather, he was simply fascinated by the whole standardized testing phenomenon. So he took various tests multiple times just to see how the tests would differ over time and how different techniques of test-taking might affect his scores. In other words, he "played" with the exams. He was a standardized test taker who bit back. One can only wonder how his various scores were "interpreted" by the test-givers and accounted for in their regional and national scoring analyses.

Deep Biases

The challenges to objective science and objective testing run still deeper. Biases are not only inescapable; they are *necessary*. Without certain beliefs, scientific inquiry simply can't be done. Nicholas Wolterstorff, an emeritus philosophy professor at Yale and a former president of the American Philosophical Association, argued in his brilliant little book, *Reason within the Bounds of Religion* (a fun twist on Kant's famous title, *Religion within the Bounds of Reason*), that science and theorizing stand on certain key beliefs or assumptions. Those beliefs are not *based on* "science," and indeed they cannot be, but they are *necessary for doing science* and theorizing. He identified three such beliefs, three such deep *biases*: Data beliefs, data-background beliefs, and what he called "control beliefs."

Very early in any research process, researchers must commit themselves to certain **data beliefs**, that is, beliefs about what they regard as constituting legitimate, appropriate data for their study (and what they regard as illegitimate or inappropriate). Before their study can begin, they must *believe* that they will be looking at the right and relevant data for their study. The circular reasoning here is obvious, perhaps troubling to some, but inescapable: you cannot prove your data beliefs scientifically (that is, with empirical data) without first believing you have the right data to prove it. Data beliefs are *believed*, not proved. One may try to justify including or excluding certain kinds of data, but these justifications are themselves fundamentally not subject to proof either (they constitute another kind of belief—*data-background beliefs*, discussed below). In the standardized testing world, test makers hold definite data beliefs that guide their decisions about what subject areas *should be* tested, what kinds of questions *should be* asked, who *should be* asked, etc. The differences between the various standardized tests often reveal just how different these data beliefs really are.

Data background beliefs are those beliefs which *justify the chosen data as useful or meaningful.* The biases of any given test or research project are clearly exposed at this point. Why do standardized tests emphasize certain subjects, disciplines or "skills" ("verbal" and "quantitative" capacities, for example) and not others (such as moral inclinations, ethics, and values)? In the current, increasingly secularized academic climate, cognition and skills are given highest preference (value?), though the pedagogical and curricular justifications for them are rarely explained (beyond vague appeals to authority: "Experts were involved in developing the tests!"). Yet surely one of the key elements of a meaningful education is ethics. Without honesty, integrity and trust, any educational system will be at risk of collapse. If students are rewarded for papers they did not write, for exams they did not take, for work they did not do, then their grades, their transcripts, their certificates, or their degrees are fraudulent and meaningless. Twice in my teaching career of more than thirty years, I have faced college classrooms where about a third of the students cheated (plagiarized) on the same assignment. The cheaters' cognitive and skill levels were clearly "college-ready," as the testing industry likes to put it. But their moral, ethical, and values capacities were significantly underdeveloped or absent. They weren't yet "college-ready" ethically. Avoiding questions about values, ethics and morals does not make tests or education "value-neutral." Far from it; it makes them "value-averse" and underdeveloped in one of the key areas of child development.

The third and final set of beliefs Wolterstorff identified as inescapable for scientific research is our **control beliefs**. These are the (often unexamined) beliefs or assumptions about the way the universe "is" or how the world "works." Control beliefs relate to our foundational "worldviews." They are less about beliefs about specific things or issues and more about one's understanding of how things and issues fit together in everyday life. Our beliefs about the nature and authority of family, children, work, the state, and how they relate to one another deeply influence and inform our education-related goals, institutions, practices, and assessments.

These data, data-background, and control beliefs, taken together, constitute deep biases inherent in any research, standardized testing included. Assumptions, biases, beliefs are ever-present in human activities because we cannot crawl out of our skins or pretend we have not been influenced by our upbringing, our language and culture, our own education, and our own values and beliefs. To deny we have such assumptions, biases and beliefs is to pretend and to deceive. Having such assumptions and beliefs does not mean our biases automatically invalidate our research; but it does mean that we must take them in account and be honest with others about those biases. The persistence of the myth of objectivity makes that level of honesty and self-awareness more difficult to recognize and to admit. The myth of objectivity is itself a distorting cultural bias that few objectivists are willing to admit they have. Objectivists cannot see, or are unwilling to admit they see, the beam in their own eye.

Systemic Weaknesses
Because of the devastating criticisms of standardized testing over the past 20 years, the test makers have begun to claim less and qualify their claims more. For example, the industry has had to admit that racial biases existed in the tests for years; they have tried desperately to remove them, but socio-economic biases persist. Students from wealthier families (who can afford SAT/ACT prep courses) and from wealthier schools consistently do better than those who hail from families that lack the funds or resources to prep for the exams. The industry has had to acknowledge that the predictive value of their tests was

no better than students' high school GPAs. More recently, the industry has acknowledged that the major standardized testing system has at least two other very serious systemic weaknesses.

First, the scoring scales used by an exam's designers must be consistent or stable over time. That is, they must actually *measure the same things in the same ways*, test after test, so they are comparing *apples to apples*, year after year. If they don't, the data will not be comparable; each shift in the kind of data collected or the methodologies used to collect them will make comparisons with the previous data sets less reliable. On this point, the SAT and ACT exams have both been significantly revised in recent years. The reasons behind the revisions are complicated, but a statement on the SAT website suggests indirectly but clearly that the test's inherent problems are not so easily overcome.

Our Commitment
Here is The College Board's Pledge accompanying The Redesigned SAT:

> We will make the redesigned SAT the most transparent exam in the assessment field. This document is just the first in a series of efforts that will provide information about and examples of the redesigned exam as early and completely as possible so that all students will know what to

expect on the day of the test, and all other stakeholders will have a clear sense of what the test contains. What the test measures will be no mystery. How we go about measuring students' reading, writing, language, and mathematics skills will be widely known.

The exam students receive on test day will be a challenging yet appropriate and fair assessment of what they know and can do. The questions will not be tricky or obscure but will instead focus on the knowledge, skills, and understandings that matter most for college and career readiness and success. As is true of the current SAT, our extensive and intensive test development process (see Appendix A) will identify and then improve or remove questions that contain errors, more than one correct answer (or no good answer), imprecision, ambiguities, biases, or other flaws.[38]

The statement above raises a host of disturbing questions about SAT's past tests and how their recent revisions will make things any better. The redesigned SAT, they say, will be "the most transparent exam" in the field: was it not transparent before, and what about the transparency of

---

[38] College Board. "Test Specifications for the Redesigned SAT." 2015.

other tests? "What the test measures will be no mystery:" that suggests they once were. Why? How SAT goes about measuring students' skills "will be widely known." Again, this suggests that they were not widely known previously. Why? The new exam will be "a challenging yet appropriate and fair assessment." To what extent were the older exams not challenging, appropriate or fair? "Questions will not be tricky or obscure." That's reassuring, but why would that statement be necessary unless some questions once were tricky and obscure? And the last sentence quoted above acknowledges that the tests do, in fact, "contain errors, more than one correct answer (or no good answer), imprecision, ambiguities, biases or other flaws" that their test development team will be sure to weed out in the future. As the College Board's "pledge" and "commitment," the statement reads more like a confession than a confident appraisal of the exam's integrity and trustworthiness.

The second, inescapable systemic weakness is on the user end of the project. Parents, high school counselors, and university admissions staff must have sufficiently deep knowledge and understanding of the testing process and statistical summaries of the data to interpret and use the scores properly and meaningfully. They must have enough expertise to understand what the tests can actually tell them and what they cannot. In other words, the users or the interpreters of the exam results must be sufficiently trained and equipped to evaluate and to interpret the test scores, lest they misread them or distort their meaning and significance. Two ACT employees acknowledged the problem this way:

> ...[I]t can take years for users to develop a deep knowledge and understanding of what the scores mean in terms of student achievement—what a student with a given score can and cannot do. And if the score scale is unstable, users may never be able to understand what scores mean.[39]

In other words, the knowledge and training the ACT team says it takes to be able to understand and to interpret its test takes years to acquire, even if the data sets are consistent and stable over time. Very few "users" of the standardized tests have that level of expertise or the time to develop such expertise. So between the recent revisions to both of the major exams and the common lack of adequate expertise in schools and universities to interpret the exams, "users may never be able to understand what scores mean." That is a deep and potentially fatal flaw to these standardized tests.

---

[39] Camara, W, Harris, D. "Why Scores on the ACT Test are Scores You Can Trust". 6 August 2016. <http://www.act.org/content/dam/act/unsecured/documents/Scores-You-Can-Trust.pdf>.

Perhaps the most significant recent acknowledgment of weakness in the dominant standardized test industry is its recognition that the tests cannot be meaningful as single measures of student learning. Again, the ACT team put it this way:

> While our research shows that ACT solutions independently measure key components of college and career readiness, we and others have begun to realize that no single solution can measure the full breadth of this readiness, nor should it. Simply put, the ACT alone is not enough to measure the full breadth of career readiness. A more holistic assessment model, incorporating multiple domains and specific skills associated with career clusters or occupations, will typically be most appropriate for describing and evaluating student readiness for college and career.[40]

That is a significant confession of weakness: a standardized test cannot "measure the full breadth" of student readiness and "a more holistic assessment" that includes many different kinds of evaluations and data is "most appropriate for describing and evaluating student readiness for college and career." Perhaps put another

---

[40] ACT. *The Condition of College and Career Readiness: National.* Iowa City, IA: American College Testing, 2016, p. 17.

way, standardized tests cannot do what they once claimed they could do and they cannot do it "objectively." But that doesn't mean they plan to go away anytime soon. Thanks to the myth of objectivity, they will continue to tread softly all the way to the bank.

The Myth of Objectivity and Standardized Testing

Calling something a "myth" is not necessarily to malign it, as the venerable Oxford Dictionary defines the term, by associating it with some of the ancient fables primitive peoples fabricated about difficult-to-understand natural phenomena. While enlightened moderns like ourselves are all too happy to leave the definition of myth there, so that *only primitive peoples* get tarred and feathered for their silly, false beliefs, our friendly Oxford-accented lexicographers do not stop there. Recognizing that all generations are capable of bowing to the idols of their age and of their own making, they threaten to deflate our modern hubris by identifying another important meaning of the term that does, in fact, apply remarkably well to our contemporary climate and to this particular phenomenon. A myth, they write, is also rightly defined as

> A widely held, but false belief or idea:
> A misrepresentation of the truth.
> A fictitious or imaginary person or thing.

An exaggerated or idealized conception of a person or thing.[41]

It is precisely upon these points (petards?)—false belief or idea, misrepresentation of the truth, a fictitious or imaginary thing, and an exaggerated or idealized conception of a thing—that one can hoist a good many standardized test maker, their governmental fan clubs, and their unsuspecting followers. Given the enormous weight of evidence now challenging the objectivity or value-neutrality of the major standardized tests, one would think the tests would be increasingly unpopular. But the testing industry continues to grow because

> The public and professionals alike share a common misconception that test scores are objective and scientific. This faulty assumption leads to an unjustified confidence in and reliance on test scores for decision-making. This means that judgments about children are based on faulty data rather than data which reflect each child's personal course of development.[42]

---

[41] "Myth". 6 August 2016. <http://www.oxforddictionaries.com/us/definition/american_englis h/myth>.
[42] Southern Early Childhood Association Position Statement. "Assessing Development and Learning in Young Children." 1996, 2000.

Alfie Kohn, author of *The Case Against Standardized Testing: Raising the Scores, Ruining the Schools* (2000), nicely sums up the problems of standardized testing and their dependence on the myth of objectivity this way:

> ...[D]on't we need an objective measure of achievement? This question is much more complicated than it may appear. Is objectivity really a desirable— or a realistic—goal? Presumably, an "objective" assessment is one that's not dependent on subjective factors such as the beliefs and values of different individuals; everyone would have to agree that something was good or bad. But disagreement is a fact of life, and it isn't necessarily something to be transcended. You and I will inevitably differ in our judgments about politics and ethics, about the quality of the movies we see and the meals we eat. It is odd and troubling that in educating our children "we expect a different standard of assessment than is normal in the rest of our lives." Too much standardization suggests an effort to pretend that evaluations aren't ultimately judgments, that subjectivity can be overcome. This is a dangerous illusion.

The quest for objectivity may lead us to measure students on the basis of criteria that are a lot less important. For the sake of the argument, though, let's assume that objective assessments are both possible and desirable. The critical point is that standardized tests do not provide such objectivity.[43]

[43] Kohn, A. *The case against standardized testing: raising the scores, ruining the schools* Heinemann, 2000

6

By What Standard?

Brian G. Daigle

Brian Daigle is headmaster and teacher at Sequitur Classical Academy in Baton Rouge, Louisiana. He is currently serving as Executive Director of Development for the Classic Learning Test, and is president of and author at Mud House Art and Literature. Brian received his Bachelor of Science degree from the School of Architecture and Design at the University of Louisiana-Lafayette and his Master of Humanities degree from the University of Dallas. His graduate work includes courses toward a Master of Arts in Trinitarian Theology and Culture from New Saint Andrews College and doctoral coursework at Louisiana State University in comparative literature. Brian is editor of the G.K. Chesterton Signature Series and author of several books, including *Street-Fighting Logic: The Art of Arguing with Grandmothers and Coffeeshop Philosophers.*

> But it is the whole definition and dignity of man that in social matters we must actually find the cure before we find the disease. (G.K. Chesterton, *What's Wrong with the World)*

The education landscape in America is a mess. It is a Jackson Pollock; it is really no landscape at all. It is a wasteland. And like all wastelands, it is ripe to be burned over and revived. Our cultural memory has evaporated. Our theological convictions have deteriorated. Our academic sensibilities are anything but academic, and they are certainly not sensible. Like all unfaithfulness, our academic unfaithfulness has had mass casualties. True to the art and biology of our day, where we are convinced that the library urinal may be called high art just as quickly as we call it a low life form, so our academic definitions have run aground. We are not sure if progress is regress, and we cannot assure our pupils that what our academic institutions offer is anything other than smoke and mirrors, smoke in mirrors, smoking mirrors, or smoky mares. At best, research has become perpetual re-search. And until we root ourselves near fresher streams, we will continue to wither.

One of those areas of academic casualties is standardized testing, college admissions tests taken widely and anxiously by most high school students aspiring to attend a college or university. But today's college admission tests have all the marks of modern education: secular, shallow, sterile, soulless, and spurious. Today's standardized tests and widespread academic measurements have all the marks of not being any worthy standard for those who are said to have been educated.

A Starting Point

When we set a boundary, we begin with principles, with ideas. And just as ideas have consequences, so standards have premises. When we build a wall, formulate a model, or set a measuring stick, we must do so because we first had a *purpose* for the wall, a *reason* for the model, or a *unit of measurement* for our measuring stick. A test is said to standardize when it brings everyone in accordance with a standard, or holds a standard up to all who enter; those in authority then explicate a student's relationship to that standard and the student's worthiness to "pass Go and collect $200." This entire book, and specifically this chapter, is a strong pursuit of questioning our assumed academic standards, especially on college entrance exams. If the world, as N.D. Wilson says, is beautiful but badly broken, then our current academic standards, and our assumptions of standardized tests, are decadent and sorely untrustworthy.

Because a discussion on education theory is most certainly a social inquiry, it is a temptation in this kind of chapter to do what Chesterton says most modern social inquiry does: "It begins as a rule with an analysis, with statistics, tables of population, decrease of crime among Congregationalists, growth of hysteria among policemen, and similar ascertained facts; it ends with a chapter that is generally called 'The Remedy.'"[44] Following that shape, this chapter would likewise begin with analyzing colleges and universities, giving statistics on job placement and average earnings from college graduates, decrease of crime among educated minorities, growth of hysteria among professors or CEOs, rising student debt, and similar ascertained facts, all by someone who is most certainly a doctor of something and who most certainly uses the term "latest research" more than they should. I would then end with a section called "Fixing the Standard." "But," as Chesterton continues, "it is the whole definition and dignity of man that in social matters we must actually find the cure before we find the disease." So it is with academic matters. Our starting point, paradoxically, must be where we intend to end. We now enter the realm of ideals, a pervasive and unavoidable pursuit in which we all must participate.

> But exactly the whole difficulty in our public problems is that some men are aiming at cures which other men would regard as worse maladies; are offering ultimate conditions as states of health

---

[44] *What's Wrong with the World*, G.K. Chesterton, page 15

> which others would uncompromisingly call states of disease...This is the arresting and dominant fact about modern social discussion; that the quarrel is not merely about the difficulties, but about the aim.[45]

The next and necessary step is no surprise: what is the purpose of an educated man or woman? Follow this question upstream, and we find an even more basic question: what's the purpose of existence, of anything whatsoever? Only when we have answered *that* correctly can we set aright our academic boundaries, the shape and design of higher and grade-school education, and therefore understand the kind of tests our students should take, along with the purpose of such tests.

> The only way to discuss the social evil is to get at once to the social ideal.[46]

But how can we? How can we begin to answer the question of ideals and standards when that requires philosophical horsepower, theological maturity, epistemological objectivity, and dialogue that is quantitatively and qualitatively more than a social media post? In short, how can we participate in such an academic exercise as determining the best academic ideal

---

[45] Ibid., page 17
[46] Ibid.

when the very foundation of the academy has eroded away, when we have lost a true academic ability to understand the history and purpose of the university and the nuances of 21st century society?

We are ill-equipped at every level and department of academia to set standards because we are ill-equipped at every level of academia to do the work required *before* we set standards. Consider for a moment the basic assumption of nearly all modern education standards: learning can and should be quantifiably measured. Consider other assumptions and practices: accumulation of course credits over students becoming credible authorities, the technical over *techne*, dogmatism over dogma, political correctness over correct, self-expression over expressing the truth, multi-culturalism over maturing culture, and progressivism over progress. We may also throw in an unveiling of another basic assumption of prevailing standardized tests: learning can be tested with multiple-choice questions. What is the true test of a learned man? Is it a test at all? What is a good and reliable assessment for those wanting to pursue their studies at a "higher" academic institution? What Chesterton says of his own inquiry into what's wrong with the world may be said of what's ultimately wrong with modern education specifically: "What is wrong is that we do not ask what is right."[47]

---

[47] Ibid.

What is the Standard for Standards?

This chapter is titled "By What Standard?" It could have just as easily been titled "By *Whose* Standard?" It is not just our standards that are broken, but our standards for setting standards. Ultimately, we wed ourselves to standard-setting authorities which have no authority. Or even worse, we participate in an academic discipline and deny we have any philosophical or theological allegiances; we lie to ourselves concerning our neutrality. But as John Milbank rightly states, "...the necessity of an ultimate organizing logic cannot be wished away."[48]

If our academic standards are broken, and education is one of the basic disciplines of being human, than we must see that the foundation of our standards is broken. If we do not know what it means to be educated, it is because we do not know what it means to be human.

Standards require ultimate authorities. They require lasting, universal, and transcendent authorities, especially when it comes to education standards. And, as stated, they require those authorities to have ideals about questions further upstream. The question of ultimate standards is one that not only impacts *making* a standardized test; it likewise informs our ability to *critique* standardized tests, *change* standardizes tests, *discuss* standardized tests, and *prepare* students for standardized tests. Therefore, by what standard do we reform

---

[48] Milbank, John. *Theology and Social Theory: Beyond Secular Reason.* Oxford, UK: Blackwell Pub, 2006, p. 1

education in general? If man is the measure of all things, as is at least functionally professed today at all levels of education, then we will only get so far as mankind will carry us.

In a discussion of standards, we ought to ask, "For what do we aim?" We must also consider where standards are best implemented and where they are best formed. Modern education—because of its dependence on the state as the most responsible agent for raising children—places the burden of forming standards on the shoulders of grade-school institutions. This also has to do with the kind of standard we recognize. The best preparation for the best higher education starts long before high school. It starts long before one's formal education. Likewise, preparation for success on any standardized test starts long before the student steps into a test prep class. A good general education begins at birth; a student's most important classroom is therefore the home. The academic tone and tempo of the home will be the foundation and framework onto which future academic endeavors are built. A home's habits of language, communication, reading, studying, and writing are the most formative for preparing a student to study at the college level.

> [A child's] character is forming under a principle, not of choice, but of nurture. The spirit of the house is breathed into his nature, day by day. The anger and gentleness, the fretfulness and

patience—the appetites, passions, and manners—
all the variant moods of feeling exhibited around
him, pass into him as impressions, and become
seeds of character in him; not because the parents
will, but because it must be so, whether they will
or not. They propagate their own evil in the child,
not by design, but under a law of moral
infection...The spirit of the house is in the
members of the children by nurture, not by
teaching, not by any attempt to communicate the
same, but because it is the air the children
breathe.[49]

Ending Where We Started
If we overcome today's beguiling but broken academic
standards—quantitative grading, standardized testing,
dual enrollment, professed religious neutrality, STEM,
magnet schools, secular scientific humanism, and
government dependence—we will be at the beginning of
a new era, a much-needed academic and societal
renaissance. We will be on the road to truly educating our
children and citizens. This is happening in many
flourishing pockets throughout the United States, and is
now moving into Canada, China, and parts of the Middle
East. The starting point to fixing our academic ills is

---

[49] Bushnell, Horace. *Christian Nurture*. New Haven: Yale Univ.
Press, 1967.

already among us because it gets the *telos* right: classical Christian education, and the many nourishing streams coming from that river, like the Classic Learning Test.

In order to build a reliable standard, we must build upon the right foundation. Again, in order to aim at having a measuring stick, we must ensure our measuring stick measures what it ought to measure and how it ought to be measured. And how can this happen without dealing with first principles, worldviews, presuppositions, ideals, clean debates, and all-around basic education—teaching a human to think well, speak well, listen well, write well, read well, and love what he ought to love? We must do this from the beginning if we wish to end in the right place:

> ...the potentiality of a philosophy cannot exceed is presupposition. What a philosophy assumes to begin with, ultimately determines all that it can be or can know.[50]

Therefore, at every level of academics and in every crevice, there must be a swift and robust return to those academic disciplines which are of primary importance in helping us answer the question, "What is the chief end of man?" We must return to theology, philosophy, poetry, history,

---

[50] Rushdoony, Rousas J. *By What Standard?: An Analysis of the Philosophy of Cornelius Van Til*. Philadelphia: Presbyterian and Reformed Pub. Co, 1959, p. 2

music, visual and spatial arts, and politics. In a deluge of delusion, our modern academic institutions make their starting point the dealings and apparent dignity of man; they therefore end where they started: the decadence of mankind.

> The crisis of present history is the collapse of the doctrine of man prevalent in Western culture since the Renaissance, a concept that has established itself not only in Europe and North America, but is increasingly prevalent throughout the world...To a great measure the crisis of modern man, as well as the crisis of theology, can be traced to a lack of an adequate standard. The concept of economic man has collapsed because man has found it an inadequate standard for life. Man cannot live by bread alone, and the increasing ferment of modern society is a witness to this truth.[51]

---

[51] Ibid. 188

7

It's a Wonderful Education:
A Conversation about the Liberal Arts between a Parent and a President
William Fahey

William Edmund Fahey is a fellow at Thomas More College of Liberal Arts, where he serves also as the College's third president. He was educated in the United States and Scotland, and holds degrees in history, classical languages, and a doctorate in Early Christian Studies. He writes and lectures on many issues that fall under the categories of "education" and "western civilization." Dr. Fahey was formerly the founding chairman of the Department of Classical and Early Christian Studies at Christendom College, where he was also president of the Faculty Senate. He has been an Accreditation Visitor and a Visiting Team Chair for the American Academy of Liberal Education. He has held a variety of fellowships including the Richard Weaver Fellowship, the Salvatori Fellowship, a Newman Fellowship, an Earhart Fellowship, and several times held the Marguerite Eyer Wilber Fellowship under the direction of Russell Kirk. William Fahey attempts, with his wife Dr. Amy Fahey, to raise 5 children and a multitude of semi-domesticated fauna and flora in New England, where his family has resided since the early 17th century.

Scene: An autumn afternoon at a small liberal arts college. Mr. Mill stops by President Bailey's office while waiting for his son and daughter to finish their time at the College Open House.

President Bailey: Come in, come in! Mr. Mill, isn't it?

Mr. Mill: Yes. That's right. You have a good memory.

B: Well, there are certain advantages of a small college; one is knowing the names of folks. Come in. Can I offer you some tea or coffee... Also, I have some rather good cookies my wife made.

M: Well, I'll have a coffee, sure. A cookie sounds good. I hope you don't mind. You said last night parents could stop by and, well, I wanted to see if that was actually true. I've been to a number of Open Houses, and, I mean, even at a small place, a President must be pretty busy.

B: Of course, but this is the sort of thing I'm busy for, so to speak. What's on your mind, Mr. Mill? As I said, I'm not really a salesman, but I do like helping people discern what could make them happy.

M: Yes, let's start with that. I mean, *shouldn't* you sell your college? I'll be honest with you: I'm not convinced that places like this are the right place for my kids. I'm just not sure. But come on, sell me.

B: Well, Mr. Mill, if helping you to figure out what is best for you, your family, and especially your son or daughter is a form of selling, then, I suppose you may call me a salesman. I love our College, and I am committed to the ideals of a liberal arts college...

M: O.K. Let's start there. I don't get it. Pretty maple trees and nice old buildings. I like that. It's peaceful and maybe a good place for someone who wants to be a teacher. But these days? Really? We live in a dynamic and changing economy. A *technological* society. I just don't see how this is anything other than a museum. I don't mean to be rude. That's not quite what I meant, but ...

B: Mr. Mill, you are a practical and loving father. You are trying to sort out what's best for your children. I admire that.

M: Well, help me out. I am curious. You seem pretty calm and confident about all this, but what's the point? How does it help to get a job? Where are the career opportunities? Isn't this just a fairytale life? A bubble?

B: Let's start with that first question: "what's the point?" You tell me, Mr. Mill. What *is* the point? I mean, what is the point of going to college at all?

M: What? You're a college president. Don't you want everyone at your college? That's your bread and butter.

B: Actually, I want people to discern their vocations and to be happy. Some should go to college, yes. Not all. And the right college is rather important. But let's stick with your excellent question. "What's the point?" Why are you here, missing a day of work, taking your son and daughter to a college Open House? Why do you think they should even go to college?

M: Okay. Sure. I think they should go to learn things. More things than we taught them at home and than they learned in their classes. They need to get ready for life. Maybe meet somebody special. Certainly, they need to get ready for a job. To be honest, with me, that's number one. Get a job.

B: Why?

M: Excuse me?

B: Why do you want them to get a job? I am serious. Give me an explanation. What's the point of that job?

M: Well, the last time I checked you needed money to have a house, and eat, and do things. Apart from that, well, that's what we all do—we work. Are you asking why work?

B: Yes. So, let's you and I cut to the chase. "Why?" You're right. I am asking a fundamental question that most people never stop to ask: "Why?" What do you think? Why *do* you work? And if you simply say "to make money," you know how I will respond. I know that you work and you make money *for some reason*, not just for the money.

M: Well, I read part of this book about business that said all good business was about making people happy. Now that I think about it, you seem to be saying something similar about college life.

B: So, you work to be happy and help others to be happy?

M: Yes. To be honest, now that I say it, I am not sure I *am* entirely happy. At least not with the work, but I am with my family. Very. My wife and kids, and sitting on my deck. Ordinary stuff. That does make me happy. I like making a place to be happy and a place for others to be happy. Also, like you, I'm a Christian, so I should add—and I believe it—I do things to get to heaven.

There you are, President Bailey: I work to be happy, to make others happy, and to try to get to heaven. How's that?

B: Pretty good. I would say you already know more than many college presidents. Now, what's happiness? How do you know you are truly happy and not just, say, distracted with something amusing?

M: Oh boy. "How do I know what the happiness is?" I know *this*: I'm enjoying this cookie. So, how about you tell me? You're the professor.

B: Those *are* good cookies and this is decent coffee. All right, I'll give you some of my thoughts. Happiness is worth thinking about. Happiness doesn't seem just to drop on people any more than winning lottery tickets do. Although to be honest, most people seem to live their lives as though happiness will happen to them without effort or thought.

M: So, are you trying to say that people who go to little liberal arts colleges are just happier?

B: I've spent a good part of my life in the academic world. I talk with all sorts of professors—some are happy, some are miserable. To raise money for scholarships, I travel and am blessed to meet with all sorts of people:

businessmen, techies, politicians, bankers, you name it. Some are happy, some are not. I'll let you in on a secret, Mr. Mill. The happy people seem to be the ones who just stop now and then and ask questions about themselves and others. They have a kind of wonder and interest in things and people. They see themselves connected to the work, experiences, and ideas of past generations. They read—some a lot, and some only a little—and they all understand this: life must be examined and lived thoughtfully with some high sense of purpose in mind. True happiness comes at the end, but along the way, thinking about what you are doing, trying to do it well, and having an informed sense of your fellow man, the world, human creativity—that broad base of knowledge and that willingness to think about life, *that* seems to offer the best chance at happiness. But happiness is a big project which involves a fair bit of self-awareness over a long period of time.

M: I agree. I wish someone had put it like that to me thirty years ago. But, look, why a little college? Why the liberal arts?

B: Well, as I said, most of the great people I have met are readers. At some point in their early adult life—typically in college—they had the opportunity to read and discuss great ideas. They saw their own experiences foreshadowed, in a way, by the experiences in literature, history and philosophy. It gave them a chance to understand themselves a little better and prepare for life. But let me ask you a serious question. Your son's and daughter's applications both indicate you have already been visiting colleges and universities—some of them big, famous places. Has anyone said anything at all about human happiness, living a whole life well, or getting to heaven?

M: No way. Certainly not heaven. They talk vaguely about success and opportunities.

B: And those are important, but too important to talk about vaguely, wouldn't you say?

M: Yes, but let's just come back to planet earth. I have real concerns. OK. Let's suppose that I am open to liberal education in a way I wasn't before. But help me out with the specifics. Address some of my concerns. We only have a little time.

B: Yes. But I am not going to give you a pass on the fundamentals without making sure we are both clear. So, you are looking at big, prestigious places that do not even talk about those things you hold most dearly and want for your children.

M: They don't talk about them directly, for sure, but look, how about my kids have a good long talk from me and my wife and then I hand them some decent books—maybe ones you recommend—on how to be happy? And then we send them off to a place with a lot of opportunities.

B: In your heart of hearts, Mr. Mill, do you believe that that will that work? When you walked around those campuses and went in those dorms, did you see truly happy people?

M: No. It was pretty wild, some of the things I saw on campus—on posters; the clubs and all that. No. And to be honest, a lot of those kids did not look particularly healthy.

B: I don't doubt, Mr. Mill, that there are good men and women, trying to do some good at those places, but a book here and a decent mentor there doesn't work at college any more than it will in the workplace or in politics. If you attempt to live a disintegrated life—I go to church over here; I party over there; I study over here; I sleep around over there—you get what you're striving for, a disintegrated life. But life doesn't like division. Sooner or later one side wins.

M: Yeah. It didn't look like the best side was winning in some of those dorms. But look, walk me through the practicals. You don't need to tell me the dorms are better at your college; clearly they are.

B: Why? Why do you say they are better?

M: First, you're committed to a Christian identity. That makes a huge difference. I'm not sure beyond on that.

B: Well, look, I have your son's file right here. He has a big-name Catholic university down as a place he visited. How was it? Christian? Wholesome?

M: Absolutely not. It actually bothered me more than the state universities we visited. But, hey, this is the real world, right? They do have name value and opportunities. They deliver success. How else are my children going to have an impact in this country?

B: You don't need to answer this question, but I will set it before you anyway: Is it worth risking your son or daughter losing, say, his or her soul, or psychological health... over a name, a nice ring on graduation day, and the promise of a lucrative job? I have a daughter in college, like you. I had to think through this, too. Simple thought experiment: Look into the future: has she gained more than she lost after four years in those dorms? Did they support her quest for true and inspiring things? You needn't answer.

M: You know I don't have to. You and I are thinking the same thing. But, really, *this* place is so small.

B: I'm not making an argument for this particular place. As I said, my college would need to be the right college for your son or daughter. I'm making an argument for what you just suggested: small.

M: What?

B: Small size. To be honest, I think all real liberal arts colleges should be small: Bold statement? Maybe. Consider this: just before, we were talking about happiness and the ability to understand what a human life is—a good one and a bad one. That's the business of what we call "the humanities," which is the heart of a liberal arts education. Books are crucial; they are the tried wisdom of the ages, but a lived community conversing about those great ideas is crucial, too. And a small community is best, if only because it is the only kind of community that can be known, lived in, and understood as one thing. It's the only kind of thing we can direct our affections toward.

M: Excuse me, I really do think this campus is very, very tranquil; I like the natural order to things; people seem happy and are friendly, but I remind you that you are less than an hour away from a major city and your own brochures talk about going to museums and seeing historic sites and shops, etc. That city has a lot of people.

B: Yes. We were talking about a college. I'm not against a big city for certain things. Not at all. As in business, there is the matter of scale. But I am talking about a community that helps form you and that provides the space to live a good, safe life, to talk, and to make friends. Do know much about anthropology?

M: No.

B: All right, what about Facebook or LinkedIn?

M: Yes, of course.

B: How many "friends" do you have?

M: My account says more than 500, but, really, I probably stay in touch, let's see, counting family, friends, and important business contacts, I don't know, I would say...

B: 150?

M: That's just what I was going say. How'd you guess?

B: Well, the median number of active contacts in social media is 200, and we don't even use all those. 150 is known as "Dunbar's Number." "What is Dunbar's Number?" you're thinking. Dunbar was an anthropologist. He studied real human communities in history and around the world. He argues pretty persuasively that the human brain—let's just say the human person—handles relationships with about 150 people pretty well. The normal human likes that number. Traditional communities were about that size; so were Roman military units and old social clubs. Really, just about anything that was considered meaningful ranged between 100 and 200 participants, optimally.

M: Interesting. Well, I have to admit I don't even think I enjoy hanging around that many people, but you're talking about a community that supports my happiness, right? But let's stick with college. Are you completely serious? A college should be small—that small?

B: I wholeheartedly believe that it should be that small, or it should be in a loose confederation of little colleges banding together into a university—like Oxford or the University of St. Andrews, which...

M: But this is America. We aren't in the Middle Ages. We are living right now.

B: Let me present you with two lists. You tell me which list, which all-star team, as it were, is more to your liking: more successful in the terms that you understand them. I will try to mix it up in both cases, so we have all kinds of people.

M: Okay.

B: First list: Alexander Hamilton, Thomas More, John Adams, Thomas Aquinas, Nathaniel Hawthorne, Robert Frost....

M: Wait, wait, you're just going to make a list of people from the past. I can see what the other list is going to be like.

B: Well, that's an interesting observation. Maybe some things were sorted out well in the past. Let's take the American founding, since you are interested in America. Picture the list of signatures on the Declaration of Independence. Many of those men were college men; all those colleges were quite small, perhaps 100, some smaller. Fairly big task, founding a republic. Fairly capable men. Picture in your mind the other list... well, take your pick of today's crowd of politicians and talking heads. Almost all educated at very large, very expensive universities, which offered no end of opportunities.

M: Seriously? Places were as small as *this* college in the past?

B. Mr. Mill, until the after the Second World War, the majority of colleges were quite small—in the hundreds, not the thousands.

M: Look, I just need to get this out there: Science. Science and Technology. You can't really compete or do much with a liberal arts background. Maybe a little, but you need to get with the STEM program and follow through. Liberal arts majors just don't contribute.

B: Do you have a laptop?

M: Yes, an HP.

B: I was hoping you would say that. David Packard was a Greek and Latin major.

M: Are you serious? But small schools, really? Small colleges can produce leaders in science or technology? You need labs and infrastructure for all the training, surely.

B: Ever send an email attachment? If you have, then thank Nathaniel Borenstein, who attended a liberal arts college that has maintained a student body of about 24 over the past several decades. LED lights? Thank Roland Winston, who went through a Great Books program at a tiny college about the size of this one. The graduates of my college? Physicians, techies, investment brokers, military intelligence officers, nurses... in addition to teaching, serving the Church, and making homes that really matter.

M: You have to be kidding me.

B: Mr. Mill, I am not against specialization or research or advanced training, but all that is best learned at the right moment, and that moment is not at the undergraduate level. Young men and women are maturing, trying to figure out who they are, and they really have a lot of basic knowledge still to discover about the world and about mankind. More importantly, young men and women need to be confronted with their own lives—the fact that their lives matter and that only they can live those lives. In a liberal arts program that confrontation and reflection happens through conversations about the greatest works of civilization. The best minds reach across the centuries and speak to young minds, forming their minds. Don't you want what is good, beautiful, tried, true, and best? The undergraduate years are about acquiring the independent habits of a disciplined mind and, at a Christian college, being formed in moral virtue—putting on the mind of Christ.

M: Yes, but what about STEM, what about everything they need? They can't even take a standardized test to get into college without a massive amount of math and science.

B: Says who?

M: Well, the STEM people. The guidance counselors and the local government. It's all changed. Everyone is saying these things—you know that.

B: Oh, I do. And I believe it is a big scam.

M: What?

B: Oh, I am exaggerating a little. I said that the world needs science and technology. Science is fascinating. I am reading a great book right now about the origins of modern science called *The Lagoon*... but to the point, STEM is not about promoting science or technology. Western Civilization seems to have made it this far and developed some wonderful things without STEM or rigged tests. These things are not, not, *not* about learning or science or real education, and they certainly are not about the well-being of your son or daughter.

M: What on earth are they about, then?

B: Money and politics—specifically, social control.

M: Oh, come on.

B: Look, each year we—you and I and all the other taxpayers—spend over $4 billion dollars on STEM-related initiatives and we have for a number of years. Have you noticed a big change in science or technology that wasn't there before? Have you seen any new opportunities for your son or daughter? That money is just another way to fund certain kinds of universities for certain kinds of people. We were told that STEM initiatives would improve things for minorities, improve test scores for the average American student, and create more teachers and greater opportunities for all. Over $4 billion each year, test results are still low, and nothing has changed, apart from the testing methods and the enrichment of already rich institutions.

M: Well, we need our society to fund research, right?

B: It wasn't doing that before? Why not just say what you're doing and why? Why dress it up as helping students, minorities, etc.? Why coordinate all of education to support STEM? To feed STEM and already rich STEM institutions? Again, who are these "STEM people" as you called them? Who promotes all this?

M: Well the testing materials come from ... the testing services companies.

B: Anyone else?

M: A lot of politicians. They have done a good job exposing the outrageous costs of education, and the big problem of student debt. They seem genuine in wanting to make education accessible for more people. Affordable.

B: These politicians who are using over $4 billion a year of tax money are trying to help us save money?

M: Okay. That doesn't make sense. Then what's going on?

B: Well, you said these same people are exposing the so-called high cost of education and at the same time promoting a solution. What is their solution?

M: Cheap community colleges. Some politicians are saying education ought to be free.

B: What kind of education? Who controls it? Will *my* college provide free education?

M: No. You would be forced out of business...Hmm. State education. It revolves around increasing access to free state colleges and universities.

B: Free?

M: Okay. Wow. So, the Federal government is funneling billions into the state university system, and all sorts of politicians are calling for subsidizing state schools—that's going to create a monopoly and crush independent and Christian schools. Wow. I never saw that.

B: It's worse than that. Those testing services—the SAT, for example—they move cheek-by-jowl with the STEM and Common Core folks for a reason. The more folks in the lottery, the more money for them, too. After all, they charge you for the test and when your child is nervous they charge another fee to cancel out the mailing of that test. And for another fee, they "help" him or her take the test again and start the billing cycle all over. The only way the test scores improve is when they "recalibrate" them. And, by the way, these so-called educational service companies are also selling your children's identity to the big schools so that your kids are recruited into the system.

M: What?

B: Yes. My college can pay to participate in that as well, but we don't. The big corporations behind those tests have created quite a financial racket and they make their money coming and going. Haven't you noticed how within weeks of taking even the pre-test—another racket—you started getting glossy mailings and emails from universities and testing services that you never heard of?

M: Well, yes.

B: It's a coordinated funnel, Mr. Mill, which pulls the sons and daughters of our country to the same end: being a cog in the system. The worst part of it, in my view, is that first matter we were talking about: the abhorrent nature of campus culture and the dormitories. Pretty expensive way to lose your innocence, isn't it, Mr. Mill?

B: My head is spinning.

M: Don't get me wrong. I believe that government has an important role in offering coordination and, at times, limited or focused financial support in higher education. But we are not talking about that with STEM and the conventional testing services. We are talking about social conformity and control. Read through the literature on STEM and the conventional standardized tests. You will see that what began as a university-level research initiative has moved slowly but surely deeper into the early years of education. Every child is having his or her curriculum changed to suit the needs of certain parts of the tech industry and certain sectors of our government. Many serious scientists are worried about STEM because it isn't about learning or science or helping individuals to be reflective and, perhaps, even happy. It is about handing already rich institutions more money and providing already rich industries with virtually free research facilities.

M: All right. I think I see that, but let me come back to the point of expense. Hasn't the current administration—and politicians from the other side, too—exposed the incredible expense of education and all the debt the students are burdened with?

B: Why do you think that? Again, I know I sound like a broken record, but who is saying education is too expensive?

M: Okay. Mostly politicians. Now that I think about it, mostly people who have an interest in expanding state education. But no. I don't fully buy that. I have seen newspaper articles saying that some students have $30, $40, or $50,000 in debt after they graduate. I am worried about debt for my children.

B: I worry about debt, too. You are right to be cautious. Let me just ask, will you tell your children not to buy a house after working a few years?

M: No, a house is still a decent investment.

B: What about a car?

M: Well, if they could live somewhere like this place, they might not need a car, but no; everyone buys cars and homes. Your point?

B: My point is merely this: although I am not absolutely in love with our economy, we live in a world where at times we invest with borrowed funds—as individuals and as businesses. One must be very careful and not go on a debt-spending spree. Still, we have a system of investment and improvement that is well-tested. We undertake and make use of many things which we cannot purchase up-front. Now, I don't want to treat education like some mere commodity, but student debt—the real student debt at decent schools—is a fraction of a mortgage. It is often less than a new car. Yet I don't hear these politicians and educational pundits calling upon Americans to stop owning homes and cars. My personal view is that debt should be kept to a minimum and rationally avoided if it is risky or for something frivolous. I would hardly say an education which provides the habit of mind needed for a good life is a poor investment. I do agree with you about tuition, however.

M: That it is out of control?

B: Yes, with some institutions.

M: Look, President Bailey, I need to go, but can you just set me straight on what I should be thinking through? I clearly have not approached this right. How do I help my kids—how do my wife and I think straight about all this?

B: Ask questions. Ask why tuition costs so much at these places you are thinking about. A visit to a campus should make that self-evident. Is the high tuition supporting teachers and the real needs of young people, or is it supporting big sports facilities, gigantic dorms, clubhouse-like student centers, and cushy, redundant jobs? Take a hard look. Also, remember, at the end of the day it is not about the size of the scholarship you might be offered. It is about the bottom line. Half of $60,000 a year is still $120,000 that you'll need to pay over four years. And remember, on the financial side, colleges are businesses. Are you uncomfortable when someone tries to lock you into a "deal" if only you'll sign on early? Don't you wonder about constant shifts in the bottom line of your payments when you show them a competitor's price? Be very careful.

M: Well, what about jobs? I just really worry about my son and daughter. I know they both hope to marry good people and have families, but a family requires a good, paying job. I know, I know, I want them to be happy, but...

B: Mr. Mill, the quest for a happy life requires a certain level of support. I agree. Here is the honest truth. Statistically, if your son and daughter go to a liberal arts college, they are likely to leave college and make about 10 percent less than someone who specialized. I'm not going to pretend the averages say anything else.

M: Well, 10 percent is not the end of the world, but you admit that they get off to a slow start and this is a world with a very dynamic and changing economy.

B: Yes. But the same statistics also indicate that when it comes to peak earnings and career movement, the liberal arts student beats his specializing peer. Don't look astonished. Look into most successful companies. The folks at the top had generalist training and are more often than not liberal arts majors. But all the studies for years have said the same thing: a liberal arts graduate makes a little less for the first five years, but over time he or she outstrips his specialized peers. If you really want to see your son or daughter become a driver of ideas and an entrepreneur, go with the liberal arts and encourage them to follow up with an advanced degree in whatever they have a passion for. These are the men and women who lead our country and create not only a life for their own families, but those of others. But make no mistake, I think it is best to concentrate on the well-being of each person, one at a time. History is made in hindsight.

M: Can we be sure that that those statistics will be true moving forward? It is such a rapidly changing world. How can we predict what will be important in the future—skills, ideas, that sort of thing?

B: Exactly. That is why the wisest thing you can do is encourage your son and daughter to pursue a liberal arts degree. Again, go out and read the data. Most young people will have three or four different jobs in the first ten years of their career. Over their lifetime, they may have more than a dozen serious jobs and at this point, every sector of our economy is showing high turnover. I have read that it is now normal to change your *career*, not just your job, several times throughout your life.

M: That's my own experience, now that I think about it. When I was in college, it was all about learning Japanese, getting ready for the showdown of the Cold War, and hoping for a job with the auto industry. I've worked in the restaurant business, high tech, and now financial planning.

B: Can you think of anything worse than encouraging your son or daughter to specialize prematurely and go off to attend... well, I don't need to name some of the places you've been looking at. I think you see why I love and believe in what I am doing here.

M: I do.

B: I hope this has been helpful, Mr. Mill. I see Mrs. Mill is coming up with your son and daughter now, so I will say goodbye.

Part III

Tests Have Consequences

8

Testing Drives Curriculum:
How College Entrance Exams Drive Curriculum Choice
Jennifer Courtney

Jennifer Courtney currently serves as the Parent Education Director and Curriculum Writer for Classical Conversations MultiMedia. She and her husband Tim have been home educating their four children classically since 2004. She has previously served as Director of Communications for Classical Conversations and as State Manager of Oklahoma. She is the co-author of *Classical Christian Education Made Approachable* and the *Classical Acts and Facts History Cards*. Jennifer enjoys traveling throughout Oklahoma and to other states to speak to parents about home education and the classical model. She graduated *summa cum laude* with a degree in English from Oklahoma State University. She was a Rhodes Scholar semi-finalist and a National Merit Scholar. Jennifer lives in Oklahoma with her husband and four children.

"The unexamined life is not worth living." This is a paraphrase from a Socratic dialogue and is one that classical educators almost always discuss with their students. It is time for us as a society to carefully examine our college entrance practices and the ways in which they influence our educational methods. To borrow a common phrase, we seem to have gotten the cart before the horse. In our country, we have allowed standardized testing to drive our practices in the classroom. Instead, we should set educational goals, craft student activities that meet those goals, and then design tests that will assess our progress toward those goals. This is the exact opposite of teaching to the test.

Diane Ravitch is a national education policy researcher. She has spent her career researching education issues and serving as a policy advisor for state education departments and national education leaders. Initially she was involved in two movements: school choice and accountability through testing. After many years of research, observation, and legislation, she changed her views: "Testing, I realized with dismay, had become a central preoccupation in the schools and was not just a measure but an end in itself ... Tests should follow the curriculum. They should be based on the curriculum. They should not replace it or precede it (*The Death and Life of the Great American School System: How Testing and Choice Are Undermining Education*).

Although many classical educators probably do not agree with all of her conclusions about school reform, we wholeheartedly support the idea that tests should be based on the curriculum. This change would ensure that tests accurately assess student readiness for college. In order to get the cart back behind the horse, we need to examine the goals for education so that we can then craft the proper tests. We can start by taking a look at the education industry.

It is important for all businesses to admit they are businesses. All nonprofit entities are. It is time for us to admit that colleges and universities are businesses as well. My own company, Classical Conversations (although it is also an educational ministry) is definitely a business. Perhaps the ultimate end of education businesses should not be to return value to shareholders (this is one thing that sets educational businesses apart), but there must be a return all the same. In the case of universities, I would assume that donors would like to see some return on their investments beyond that of their name on a building. They need to see good quality students entering the universities and to see the accomplishments of the graduates from those institutions. This has everything to do with evaluating current admissions processes. Colleges need students that match up well with their particular programs so that they stay and graduate, get jobs, benefit their communities, and eventually donate back to the college. This becomes a very productive cycle as the returns enhance the college's image, attract more students to apply, and ensure long-term sustainability.

It is time to consider whether the current admissions processes (relying almost exclusively on the ACT/SAT) are contributing to student selection and to education itself or are undermining those two things. Many critics of standardized testing have delved into issues of fairness, citing the class, wealth, and even race bias of the tests. Others have talked about the income gap between those who can afford expensive test preparation programs and tutors. As we look at this issue in my company, we are far more concerned with what would seem to be the most pressing questions: 1. Does standardized testing accurately predict student readiness for college? 2. Do these tests actually find the students who will contribute to the college community, and later to the wider community? 3. What are the detrimental effects on education when so much time is spent preparing students for standardized tests? What great books and conversations are being lost in this process?

Classical Conversations has been in business since 1997, and will soon be celebrating our 20th anniversary. We began as a middle school and high school program. After seeing the caliber of work that our students were prepared to do in comparison to the caliber of work we wish they had been prepared to do, we started a K4-6th program so that families would be prepared to be successful. In short, those who were seeking to join our program were not prepared for the level of work that was going to be required of them. Based on my conversation with a number of college and university professors, this seems to be a similar problem faced by them today. These schools continue to add more and more remedial classes and to "dumb down" the freshman level classes so that an acceptable number of students will be able to pass them.

As businesses, we all have an obligation to our customers to provide them a service that they want or think they want. You are probably familiar with the claim that Henry Ford famously said, "If I had asked people what they wanted, they would have said faster horses." Whether or not he ever uttered this phrase, it accurately captures the debate we all face about giving customers only what they want or creating something that they did not know they wanted. Whatever side of this debate you come down on, I am guessing that you did not ride in a horse-drawn cart to the location where you are reading this book today. I am equally sure that the ACT and SAT were two different beasts when they were first developed, but now it seems to me they are the same thing called by different names. Initially, these standalone tests were largely ignored until close to college admissions time. Many students took them only once, especially if they earned a high enough score to gain admittance to the higher learning institution of their choice. Now, families and students will pay thousands of dollars and spend years studying specifically for them. These tests have had unintended consequences, consequences which have made it difficult for colleges to use the tests for their intended purposes. We can all agree that colleges must have an economical way to successfully match students to their programs. However, what was once a single part of evaluating a student's readiness for college or their fitness for a particular college or program of study has become the only item of evaluation. What was originally one branch of the main path has become the ONLY path.

K-12 educators love the children they serve and want them to be successful, but, unfortunately, they have been conditioned that there is a single door (SAT/ACT) that leads to success. They know deep down that there are many other indications of educational success, but the pressure of the outside world (parents, administrators, curriculum providers) forces them to focus on teaching children to achieve high test scores. Although this model ostensibly makes it easier for colleges to sift through potential students and choose the best ones, it is actually driving behavior in K-12 that is detrimental to the college's success. Many colleges around the nation now find themselves in the position of having to offer remedial courses in math and English because the students who scored high enough to gain admission to their institutions were not actually prepared to study there.

Every other year, we survey the students who participate in our Classical Conversations communities.

These students routinely score in the 80-85th percentile on the SAT/ACT without studying specifically for it. In our most recent survey, 93 percent of the graduates who responded were accepted by all of the schools to which they applied with the average number of applications at 3.2 per student. This same group of students scored higher than the state and national averages in multiple subject categories of both the ACT and SAT exams (even though our programs do not focus on test preparation at all and many of these families do minimal test preparation in favor of other learning activities). In addition, our students have much higher rates of participation in church and in community service and extracurricular activities. 88 percent of the students surveyed participated in mock trial or debate, 60 percent in sports, 73 percent in music, and 67 percent in ministry. An astounding 85 percent of them participate in Bible study. Fifty-three percent of them serve as academic camp leaders for younger children during the summer training practicums we offer for homeschooling parents. Although it might be difficult to scientifically prove a direct connection, there is certainly room to note that students who do not focus solely on preparing for tests are able to devote time to music, athletics, scouting, and community service.

In addition, our students finish high school after completing an amazing reading list that familiarizes them with the best thinkers. By the time they graduate, they have read, discussed, and written essays about nineteen

American novels, nineteen British poems and novels, six Shakespeare plays, and the classics of Greece and Rome including *The Iliad*, *The Odyssey*, *The Aeneid*, and *Oedipus Rex*. Because we leave questions of test preparation in the hands of families and out of our classrooms, these students have read these novels and plays in their entirety. In addition, they have read them to learn about the best and worst actions that are possible in humanity instead of reading them to pass nationally or locally legislated literacy standards.

While standardized tests tend to focus students narrowly on reading comprehension or grammar usage, our seminars are focused on teaching students to think deeply about a wide range of issues. They think about these issues through classroom debate (all students participate in both team policy and Lincoln-Douglas debate), through courses in formal logic (by the time they graduate, most of our students have taken four courses in logic), and courses that most high schools are forced to neglect, such as philosophy and art and music history. Their reading is not limited to the classics of Western civilization. Students are also required to read, summarize, and sometimes memorize the founding documents of the United States such as the Declaration of Independence, the Constitution, and the Federalist Papers. Students study Latin for multiple years, translating Caesar, Cicero, and Virgil. Students complete hands-on science labs together in small groups and communicate their findings through formal lab reports. We prefer students to spend time reading about big ideas like ownership, discipline, freedom, choices, consequences, leadership, and duty instead of spending time learning how to "game" a standardized test. Rather than have them focus on disconnected fragments of information that will only stay with them for a season, we prefer to have them reflect on objects and ideas that lead them to truth, goodness, and beauty. We would argue that these activities are the ones that prepare students for a life of study in the university. More importantly, these activities are the ones that prepare students for a lifetime of learning and of service. Rather than educating kids who are "smart," we want to raise adults who exercise wisdom (knowing what is right) and virtue (doing what is right). The virtue of self-discipline, along with intellectual curiosity and original thinking, would seem to be the best indicator of preparedness for college.

In addition to the plethora of recent articles bemoaning the unpreparedness of high school graduates for college coursework, there have been an equal number of articles addressing the unpreparedness of college graduates for the workforce. Most of these center on the same theme: a lack of communication skills. Without delving too far into this issue, it is plain to see that our current standardized tests do nothing to encourage student preparation in the area of communication. At best, students may have to write a single essay. These essays are artificial in the sense that they do usually do not require students to access and synthesize the knowledge they have gained in high school. Rather, they encourage students to memorize or make up a few clever quotes, write a thesis statement, and make the essay long enough to satisfy the overwhelmed and underpaid graders. Even this writing practice, while better than nothing, does not assess their oral communication skills. Many students who excel at multiple guessing are unable to present themselves well in a brief speech or in a job interview.

As with any educational endeavor, it is best to start with the end in mind. In Classical Conversations, we desire to cultivate wisdom and virtue in our students, so we design our assessment according to that end goal. Rather than giving a lot of fact-based quizzes or multiple-choice exams, we ask students to write a lot of blue book exams or to deliver finals orally. In this way, we discourage the practice of cram, test, and dump with which so many of us parents are familiar from our own school days. Instead, we ask students to reflect thoughtfully on the ideas that we have encountered during the course of a semester, whether those are ideas about the justice of the death penalty or the proper definition of a hero or the advantages and disadvantages of classification systems. Not only do these exams encourage students to synthesize their lessons across the semester, but they also encourage students to synthesize their lessons across the subjects. *How is the process of classifying organisms the same and different in traditional logic as it is in biology? Using our definition of heroic action, how could you compare and contrast one of Shakespeare's characters to a Founding Father or Revolutionary War hero?* This kind of thinking and wrestling with ideas and struggling to communicate our ideas to others is what makes for better college students, better colleagues, and better human beings.

We can all agree that these are the kinds of thinking and communication skills we would wish to cultivate in our K-12 students. However, it is the very kind of thinking that is prevented by the standardized tests we use today to assess college readiness. In contrast, those tests require students to access fragmented and disconnected pieces of information from the previous three or four years of their math and science classes or to practice reading comprehension on texts which have no context (and usually no interesting content). Finally, students are encouraged not to access the knowledge they have gained in the previous four years and look at it as some kind of unified whole, each piece of which informs and illuminates the other pieces. Instead, they are encouraged to attend classes which teach them clever guessing strategies, a skill that is rarely needed in college or the workplace. All of these reasons have compelled us to steer away from this kind of testing in our Classical Conversations communities.

It is encouraging to see that more concerned educators are beginning to talk about the options for schools. Although it is time-consuming for the colleges, they could certainly design their own entrance exams as they once did. In addition, they could pay more attention to essays, resumes, and recommendations. Some are already suggesting that student GPA would be another way to assess student readiness.[52] Of course, GPA would not help the homeschoolers who are served by our company, but it is exciting to see that colleges are looking at different measures. Many of the families we serve have shared that the colleges their students attended were most impressed by the list of works they had read and thought about. Perhaps it is time for us to expand our thinking about transcripts as well. Noting that a student earned four credits in English seems paltry compared to a list of 19 American literature titles, 19 British literature titles, 6 Shakespeare plays, and so on. Too often, as a society, we have accepted the idea that truth can only be arrived at through empirical measures. However, our students are not science experiments for us to weigh, measure, and record. Rather, like us, they are complex human beings with some innate talents and some gifts that require cultivation. It is time to think about the proper ways to assess these talents. Although time-consuming, student

---

[52] http://www.pbs.org/newshour/rundown/nail-biting-standardized-testing-may-miss-mark-college-students/ Published Feb. 18, 2014, accessed Aug. 8, 2016.

interviews would give admissions offices a clear measure of the student's thinking and communication skills. A resume would give a clear indication of the balance between their traditional academic life and their enrichment or service activities. A recommendation from a supervisor would give a clear measure of their work ethic. A list of works read and studied would give a clear indication of the breadth of their knowledge and interests.

One piece of this assessment will always be testing. It is our hope that this testing could be more like the culminating exams given in historical series like *Little House on the Prairie* and *Anne of Green Gables*, among others. These were tests which assessed student knowledge in areas like algebra, geometry, and trigonometry. They were tests which assessed the student's familiarity with the English language and their facility using it. They were tests which assessed student mastery of grammar and translation in foreign languages. They were tests which assessed students' familiarity with the great classics and the ideas presented in them. It is our hope that, as classical educators, we will reshape the conversation by encouraging all educators to think first about the important ideas and skills which should comprise a K-12 education and then to design tests that will assess student mastery of those ideas and skills.

9

Test Prep that Works:
It's Not About the Test
Janice Campbell

Janice Campbell is the author of *Excellence in Literature*, a self-directed, college-prep English curriculum for grades 8-12. Among other resources for parents and students, Janice wrote *Transcripts Made Easy, Get a Jump Start on College*, now in its third edition, as a guide for helping homeschool parents grant credits to and keep clean and efficient records for their student. More of her articles may be found at DoingWhatMatters.com and her books at Everyday-Education.com.

Education is an atmosphere, a discipline, and
a life. (Charlotte Mason)[53]

By the time students take college admissions exams, they
have been engaged in test preparation for well over a
decade. No matter how they have been formally
educated—in public, private, or home schools—the
atmosphere, discipline, and life of the home has been
providing foundational preparation for both life and
testing. How can families ensure that students are
receiving what they need in order to be prepared for
college and life beyond?

First, Own Books
In suggesting that atmosphere was an important part of
education, Charlotte Mason was ahead of her time. A
2010 study on over 70,000 students in 27 nations reports
that a family's "scholarly culture—the way of life in homes
where books are numerous, esteemed, read, and enjoyed"
matters. The study measured families' scholarly culture by
the number of books in the home, and used a
comprehensive set of control variables to estimate the
effect of scholarly culture on children's education.

Consistently, across boundaries of class, race, and

---

[53] Mason, Charlotte. *Home Education* and *A Philosophy of Education*.
Reissued 1989.

gender, the study found that a book-oriented home "endows children with tools that are directly useful in learning at school," including, but not limited to:

vocabulary
information
comprehension skills
imaginative richness
broad horizons of history and geography
familiarity with good writing
understanding the importance of evidence in argument.[54]

Scholarly culture affects the educational achievement of children, "not only in the rich, long-democratic, market-oriented nations of Western Europe and its overseas extensions, but also in Eastern Europe, in Asia, in South America, and in South Africa. The effect remains strong after controlling for well-known sources of educational advantage: parents' education, father's occupation, father's class and ownership situation, gender, GDP when growing up, and nation. Moreover, the effect is strong across the whole political spectrum—in every one of our 27 countries and as far back in history as our survey

---

[54] Evans, M. D. R., et al. Family scholarly culture and educational success: Books and schooling in 27 nations. *Research in Social Stratification and Mobility* (2010), doi:10.1016/j.rssm.2010.01.002. Retrieved on: 25 August 2016, pp. 3, 19.

data can take us. It was strong in societies whose educational systems were redesigned explicitly to eliminate class privilege (Eastern Europe under Communism, China during the Cultural Revolution). It was strong among the underclass in a society designed to maintain group privilege (South African blacks under Apartheid)"[55] Even in cultures with a hostile ideological perspective, and especially for students at the bottom of the social hierarchy, scholarly culture confers skills that lead to educational success.[56] Although it may seem too simple to be true, the study clearly shows that books in the home can balance out many of the most challenging obstacles to achievement.

Enjoy Books

> The sole substitute for an experience which we have not ourselves lived through is art [and] literature ...From man to man, as he completes his brief spell on Earth, art transfers the whole weight of an unfamiliar, lifelong experience with all its burdens, its colours, its sap of life; it recreates in the flesh an unknown experience and allows us to possess it as our own.[57]

---

[55] Ibid. 17
[56] Ibid. 19
[57] Alexandr Solzhenitsyn.1970. Nobel Lecture in Literature.<http://www.nobelprize.org/nobel_prizes/literature/laure

It is not necessary or even beneficial to approach books in an academic way. Instead, the study shows that the benefits of scholarly culture were derived from simply possessing books and spontaneously and informally using them for delight, rather than simply as learning tools. Scholarly culture is an atmosphere that runs deeply through a child's entire life, creating a rich mental environment of words and ideas. As "parents give their infants toy books to play with in the bath; read stories to little children at bed-time; give books as presents to older children; talk, explain, imagine, fantasize, and play with words unceasingly," their children develop a taste for reading and thinking. They "learn the words, master the skills, buy the books."[58] Thus scholarly culture passes from one generation to the next.

In addition, the researchers suggest that a large home library demonstrates an interest in knowledge, and "suggests that conversations between parents and their children will include references to books and imaginative ideas growing out of them."[59] Families who are "reading for pleasure, acting out stories based on favorite books, playing charades or word games on a winter's night" are helping students acquire the skills and knowledge that

---

ates/1970/solzhenitsyn-lecture.html.> Retrieved on: 26 August 2016.

[58] Evans, p. 17

[59] Ibid. 4

will help them succeed, even though it may seem they are simply having fun together.[60]

In a family with a scholarly culture, language arts become much more than just a collection of skills to master. Books provide students with the ability to put life into words. As they read about the experiences of others, they are able to place their own experiences in perspective. They begin to understand the significance, beauty, or tragedy of an event in a way that is nearly impossible for a person who does not read. They learn not only to discern themes and allusions, but by example they are taught to clearly express feelings, describe experiences, and empathize with others. Literature not only teaches communication skills, it can be the basis for a worldview centered in beauty, truth, and goodness. In this way, it helps to prepare students for both life and testing.

Choose Good Books

> The task of the modern educator is not to cut down jungles but to irrigate deserts. (C.S. Lewis, *The Abolition of Man*)

Because books and reading have such a powerful impact on student success, it is important to choose well. This does not mean starting a kindergartner on Plato or

---

[60] Ibid. 2

Tolstoy; it means establishing simple habits of reading and talking about good, age-appropriate literature. In his book *The Death of Christian Culture*, Dr. John Senior suggests that since the "cultural soil has been depleted" it is necessary to cultivate "an imaginative ground saturated with fables, fairy tales, stories, rhymes and adventures; the thousand books of Grimm, Andersen, Stevenson, Dickens, Scott, Dumas, and the rest." Reading these "thousand good books" irrigates the spiritual desert, and prepares the heart and mind for great books. If older students didn't read them in childhood, it's never too late. As C. S. Lewis reminds us, "A children's story that can only be enjoyed by children is not a good children's story in the slightest."

Literacy requires that readers understand both text and subtext. A reader who encounters the name "Hamlet" without an awareness of the complex interplay of revenge, indecision, and circumstance the allusion references, misses the allusion and possibly a major point of the conversation. Like a child who feels left out and bored by adult conversation—not because it is actually boring, but because his childish ignorance deprives him of the background needed for understanding—the reader has been left behind. Contemporary writing, including journalism, is full of literary allusions that add depth and meaning—as long as they are understood. Educator E. D. Hirsch explains that "Only by accumulating shared symbols, and the shared information that the symbols represent, can we learn to communicate effectively with one another."[61] Beyond its obvious contribution to the development of communication skills, reading widely also builds historical literacy. In his 1970 address to the Nobel prize committee, Alexandr Solzhenitsyn reminds us that "World literature has it in its power to convey condensed experience from one land to another so that we might cease to be split and dazzled, that the different scales of values might be made to agree, and one nation learn correctly and concisely the true history of another with such strength of recognition and painful awareness as it had itself experienced the same, and thus might it be spared from repeating the same cruel mistakes." Literature is a powerful instrument in the quest for justice and peace.

Read to Understand

> I am cheered by a vital awareness of World Literature as of a single huge heart, beating out the cares and troubles of our world... (Alexandr Solzhenitsyn)

Good literature broadens the inner world. Without

---

[61] Hirsch, E.D. 1988. *Cultural Literacy: What Every American Needs to Know. New York*: Vintage Books. p. xvii.

literature, we live alone—caged within our own experiences. We are limited by the confines of space and time until we open the literary door to the experiences of others. We learn to empathize by experiencing the feelings of others. We learn, through vivid example, to beware of that which is false, temporal, and worthless. We learn about consequences by experiencing the suffering and joy of others. We learn to communicate from the best communicators of all time (and deep, clear communication is essential for healthy relationships).

Literature shared becomes a "living memory." It opens an arena of common space, a context within which we can move toward greater understanding of self and others. The characters and settings we encounter in literature become a vivid shorthand by which we can communicate an idea. To describe someone as a Hamlet or a Bertie Wooster offers a far more vivid picture of their personality and character than could be achieved through the use of simple adjectives. Without a common literary foundation, the meaning of the comparison evaporates. As Solzhenitsyn puts it, when a shared literary heritage is lost, a "nation ceases to be mindful of itself, it is deprived of its spiritual unity, and despite a supposedly common language, compatriots suddenly cease to understand one another."

How to Choose What to Read
Life is short, and there will always be more books than

time. Create a habit of choosing from many varieties of literature, including novels, plays, poetry, biographies, memoirs, history, and science. Especially for classic literature, consider the following questions as you select books for K-12 reading, especially as students move into middle and high school.

Is this work foundational to an understanding of Western civilization and culture?

Is it a classic work that is regularly alluded to in current conversation (including newspaper, radio, books and movies)?

Does it tell the truth about life and consequences?

Is there something compelling about this particular work that makes it, more than another, deserve a place in the curriculum?

Does it offer a unique perspective on the culture of its time and place?

Does the book have the power to engage readers and cause them to think deeply about important issues?

Is it well-written?

Has it endured the test of time?

Although it can be tempting to choose books solely because they are familiar or appealing, it is important not to base selections entirely on your preferences. Some works need to be included because of their place in the literary canon, even if you have negative memories of the book as it was presented in your own educational experience. Present the book in its historic, literary, and artistic context, and chances are that you will enjoy the selection much more than you thought possible. Favorite books and historical periods aside, remember that a good chronological overview of American, British, and world literature is foundational in order to understand the source, development, and consequences of the ideas that shaped Western culture.

Read the Bible

The scholars who produced this masterpiece are mostly unknown and unremembered. But they forged an enduring link, literary and religious, between the English-speaking people of the world. (Winston Churchill)

One of my college professors stated that the single most helpful thing an English-speaking student can read is the King James (or Douay–Rheims) Bible, and based upon my own experience in college-level literature classes and test-taking situations, I agree. Not only does it contain many of the most enduring themes of literature, its literary quality is unparalleled. Through history, wisdom literature, poetry, prophecy, and parable, it can nourish the soul while offering a window into different cultures of the past. Fascinating stories capture the imagination, while its highly sophisticated vocabulary and syntax prepares students for reading other classics. I grew up on the KJV, and my thoughts, literary imagination, and writing continue to be permeated by the rhythm and cadence of King James English.

Reading the KJV does not mean that students will begin to think of others as "thee" or "thou," or use words like "verily" or "thence." It means that when he or she meets King James English in Shakespeare's *Macbeth* or Milton's *Paradise Lost*, the language is both clear and familiar, making it possible to enjoy the story and discern themes and allusions. It means that when the student encounters references to Jonah, a lion's den, or a "Gadarene rush" in a newspaper editorial, the allusion is familiar and the student is likely to understand the thrust of the argument.

How and when should one introduce children to the King James or Douay–Rheims Bible? We started in very early childhood with our family, just as generations before us had done. We read stories and Psalms, and sometimes the boys would memorize, dramatize, or illustrate them. This helped to make the language and stories part of the everyday fabric of our lives.

Memorize and Recite

As families read, write, and think together, remember to memorize and recite poetry, scripture, drama, speeches, and important historical documents. Students and writers from Cicero to Shakespeare to C. S. Lewis memorized the epic poetry, speeches, and literature of the classical world, providing them with a wealth of words and images to draw upon in their own thinking and writing. What is memorized becomes our own, and can ever after be drawn upon for guidance, comfort, and inspiration. Charlotte Mason wrote, "Memory is the storehouse of whatever knowledge we possess; and it is upon the fact of the stores lodged in the memory that we take rank as intelligent beings." Despite modern education's preference for teaching skills rather than facts, it is at least as important to have a well-furnished mind as it is to master basic skills.

The study on scholarly culture concludes, "families matter not just for the material resources they provide, not just because of parents' formal educational skills, but also—often more importantly—because of the scholarly culture they embody."[62] Literature is the

---

[62] Evans, p. 19-20

cornerstone of that scholarly culture. It prepares students for standardized tests, to be sure, but more than that it equips them for life. As Solzhenitsyn reminds us, the reading and writing of literature is not simply a private academic exercise. Rather, it "conveys irrefutable condensed experience ... from generation to generation. Thus it becomes the living memory of the nation. Thus it preserves and kindles within itself the flame of her spent history, in a form which is safe from deformation and slander. In this way literature, together with language, protects the soul of the nation."

On the personal level, Pliny the Younger speaks vividly of the capacity of literature to enrich life when he wrote, "Literature is both my joy and my comfort; it can add to every happiness and there is no sorrow it cannot console." Great literature remains timeless and relevant because the central concerns of humanity—the purpose of life, the existence and nature of God, love, loss, change, challenge, truth, beauty, goodness—change little across the millennia. Education as an atmosphere, a discipline, and a life is test prep that is not about the test, and it begins with books in the home.

10

A Liberating Test
Andrew Seeley

For more than two decades, Dr. Andrew Seeley has been a Tutor at Thomas Aquinas College in California. A 1987 graduate of Thomas Aquinas, Dr. Seeley received his Licentiate from the Pontifical Institute in Medieval Studies (Toronto) and a Ph.D. in Medieval Studies from the University of Toronto (1995). His teaching experience includes courses in Biblical Studies, Patristics, Logic, Language, Natural Philosophy, Biology, Geometry, Cartesian Algebra, Differential Calculus, Number Theory, non-Euclidean Geometry, Ancient, Medieval and Modern Philosophy and Literature, Classical Physics and Relativity, and Music Theory. In 2005 Dr. Seeley became Executive Director at the Institute for Catholic Liberal Education. Dr. Seeley is on the National Policy Advisory Board for the Catholic High School Honor Roll, Wyoming Catholic College's Catholic Scholars Advisory Board, and a number of Catholic liberal arts schools around the country. His articles have been published online in *Crisis, First Things,* and *The Imaginative Conservative,* among others. He is co-author of *Declaration Statesmanship: A Course in American Government.* Dr. Seeley is married to Lisa Seeley and is father to six children and grandfather to three.

And if in that time there were among them
any honors, praises, and prizes for the man
who is sharpest at making out the things that
go by, and most remembers which of them
are accustomed to pass before, which after,
and which at the same time as others, and
who is thereby most able to divine what is
going to come, in your opinion would he be
desirous of them and envy those who are
honored and hold power among these
men?[63]

It is hard to overestimate the damage standardized tests
have done and are doing to our schools, our churches and
our society. Since the 2001 No Child Left Behind Act
tied federal money to school success on standardized
tests, administrators, parents, students, and teachers have
increasingly focused their efforts and anxieties toward
achieving high scores on the tests that determine whether
they will be admitted to colleges of their choice and
perhaps receive scholarships to help with costs. In my
experience, the fear that this federal push for
accountability would lead to "teaching to the test" is
abundantly justified. I hear story after story from teachers
to the effect that there is only one question now: "Will

---

[63] Plato. *The Republic.* Book VII, 516d. Translated by Allan Bloom.

this be on the test?" Students are trained to think that this is what formal learning is all about – learning to imbibe as much information as possible, retaining it long enough to pass the test, and then letting it all flow out in order to move on to prepare for the next test.

Current standardized college entrance exams reward those trained in this fashion. One widely available practice test[64] is dominated by selections that present information of little to no interest to anyone without a particular, momentary need, in language typical of textbooks or newspapers. One selection presents suggestions for making mass transportation more attractive so that society might avoid the dangers of the automobile. Another tells the story of one man's theory about the evolutionary use of a not-yet fully adapted wing. Others include popular science articles exploring the reasons for the collapse of the honeybee colony population and how the cyclopropane 1-MCP is being used to lengthen the life and increase the sweetness of apples. High scores will be achieved by those who can analyze and edit such meaningless selections.

Erica Goldson, the 2010 valedictorian at Athens-Coxsackie High School in the Albany area, used her

---

[64] Test 3 from this site:
https://collegereadiness.collegeboard.org/sat/practice/full-length-practice-tests

speech[65] to forcefully reveal how much students and teachers suffer from a de-humanizing system.

I should look at this as a positive experience, especially being at the top of my class. However, in retrospect, I cannot say that I am any more intelligent than my peers. I can attest that I am only the best at doing what I am told and working the system. Yet, here I stand, and I am supposed to be proud that I have completed this period of indoctrination....I have successfully shown that I was the best slave....And quite frankly, now I am scared.

"Now I am scared." Erica's perceptive comment reveals the extent to which the hearts and souls of students are atrophied and warped by the dominance of the test. The best test-takers tend to be those who simplify all distracting considerations, refusing to linger over anything in their studies that might engage their attention. They understandably focus on the words they need to commit to memory, not on the images and experiences that give those words reality.

Some of you may be thinking, "Well, if you pass a test, or become valedictorian, didn't you learn

---

[65] http://americaviaerica.blogspot.com/2010/07/coxsackie-athens-valedictorian-speech.html

something?" Well, yes, you learned something, but not all that you could have. Perhaps, you only learned how to memorize names, places, and dates to later on forget in order to clear your mind for the next test.

What effect does this excessive obsession with empty words have on persons trapped within the school cave? Can one flourish in life or work without learning to focus attentively on the images and realities signified by the words? How will society fare as more and more of those simply trained to take tests become doctors and bank managers and political leaders, not to mention teachers?

One professor of physical therapy told me how classes had devolved from an exciting challenge driven by the questions of motivated students to a vain labor to get his students to ask more than the one question. "Physical therapy is not a test!" he urges. A therapist needs to analyze each patient. He needs to know how to ask the questions, so that he might find out about their illness and history, but even more so that he might learn about his patients – how much therapy do they need, how much will they will be able to take, how much will they do on their own. The only important test they will experience after they graduate from the artificial environment of the university is whether their patients return to full health and mobility.

Today's situation is a further step in a devolution already well underway in the twentieth century, when schools abandoned traditional liberal arts education in favor of that which would seemingly give them a leg up in pursuing a career. In a 1947 Oxford speech[66] that eventually spawned the American classical liberal arts movement, writer Dorothy Sayers decried the effect of an educational system that taught each subject as though it were its own world, and paid no attention to the overall development of students as learners.

> Although we often succeed in teaching our pupils "subjects," we fail lamentably on the whole in teaching them how to think: they learn everything, except the art of learning. It is as though we had taught a child, mechanically and by rule of thumb, to play "The Harmonious Blacksmith" upon the piano, but had never taught him the scale or how to read music; so that, having memorized "The Harmonious Blacksmith," he still had not the faintest notion how to proceed from that to tackle "The Last Rose of Summer."

This approach ensured that students stuffed with facts pertaining to history or chemistry or even religion had never developed their ability and appetite to learn new

---

[66] http://www.gbt.org/text/sayers.html

things. They never learned how to think clearly or to speak powerfully. Sayers believed that this made for youth and adults prone to emotional manipulation through the words and images pouring in from radio and television. She blamed the terrible war Britain and the rest of the world had just barely survived in part on a populace which could not ascribe meaning to what they experienced.

> They do not know what the words mean; they do not know how to ward them off or blunt their edge or fling them back; they are a prey to words in their emotions instead of being the masters of them in their intellects. We who were scandalized in 1940 when men were sent to fight armored tanks with rifles, are not scandalized when young men and women are sent into the world to fight massed propaganda with a smattering of "subjects;" and when whole classes and whole nations become hypnotized by the arts of the spell binder, we have the impudence to be astonished.

Now even individual subjects have lost their intrinsic charm. They are only mastered to the extent needed to pass the test given by the teacher or by the testing corporation. Oftentimes it seems that colleges have bought into this mentality. What kinds of students do they want to admit? What kinds do they want to honor and support through scholarships? Those that have made themselves into high-achieving, test-taking slaves?

Some colleges and universities are recognizing the detrimental effects of the "test for success" culture. They want students who have richer experiences in high school, and show depth rather than breadth. Many either have or are considering dropping the standardized test as a required part of the admissions process. And many parents, forced to take their children's education into their own hands, have felt frustrated at standardized tests that favor students who have never tasted the serious education they have tried to provide themselves through homeschooling or helping found charter or independent schools. As Jeremy Tate, CEO of the Classic Learning Test, states,

> The truth is that the current college entrance exams reflect a philosophy of education that is often at odds with parents' deepest convictions. These parents believe that religion, logic, ethics, and philosophy are the most important courses for their child as these disciplines form a person in specific and important ways. When these parents prepare their children for arguably the most important test they will ever take, shouldn't this test also affirm the values they hold most dear?

The Classic Learning Test is a response to the demands for a standardized test that provides some measure of the success of richly humane education. In stark contrast to other test options, reading through the CLT practice test is a delight for a serious reader. C.S. Lewis reveals the moral dangers of wanting to become part of the "Inner Ring" in any organization. Flannery O'Connor presents shifty Mr. Shiftlet and signs of danger missed by two lonely women. St. Augustine answers a difficult question about the importance of keeping oaths. John Paul II explains the significance of the life and death of Edith Stein. Great authors writing about topics of great substance.

The CLT is truly classical in spirit. In an essay[67] which formed part of his *Idea of a University*, John Henry Newman, one the greatest authors of nineteenth century England, explained the principles behind the entrance examinations for the university he founded in Dublin. These oral examinations sought to determine how well potential university students could read the works of the greatest authors. Newman gives two lengthy imagined examples of such examinations. Writing several generations before Sayers, Newman believed that a proper education should change students in a lasting way. They should be able to look carefully at the details of anything put before them, judge their intrinsic

---

[67] http://www.newmanreader.org/works/idea/article4.html

importance, and express their own thoughts carefully and precisely.

> One main portion of intellectual education, of the labours of both school and university, is to remove the original dimness of the mind's eye; to strengthen and perfect its vision; to enable it to look out into the world right forward, steadily and truly; to give the mind clearness, accuracy, precision; to enable it to use words aright, to understand what it says, to conceive justly what it thinks about, to abstract, compare, analyze, divide, define, and reason, correctly.

The entrance examination aimed to determine:

> Whether he understands how the separate portions of a sentence hang together, how they form a whole, how each has its own place in the government of it, what are the peculiarities of construction or the idiomatic expressions in it proper to the language in which it is written, what is the precise meaning of its terms, and what the history of their formation.

The student was measured by his ability to understand completely the expressions of the greatest writers in history, something he could only do to the extent that he used the words to make ideas of the authors his own. Newman's first example shows a young man being quizzed on the meaning of the word, "Anabasis," which forms the title of Xenophon's account of the Greek army that marched 1000 miles through enemy territory to get home. Newman highlights his inability to analyze the word into its roots and forms, and to understand the significance of the title with respect to the whole work, which shows that he has not developed his mental capabilities to be a serious lifelong learner. In the second example, Newman shows a young man reading from one of Cicero's letters who is able, when questioned, to explain the form of any word and the role it plays in the sentence, to recall the range of its possible meanings and the one most likely in the context, to consider other words Cicero might have used but didn't, and why he might have chosen the one he did in the light of his audience and subject. Further, the student could readily understand the questions the examiner put to him to push his analysis further, and assess and adapt to the suggestions the examiner made to him.

Newman thought that a proven ability to engage seriously and carefully with the greatest authors provided universities, students and parents with a sure hope for future success. He also believed, along with Dorothy Sayers and those involved in today's liberal arts revival, that such students are the best prepared to discover satisfying lives and provide needed societal leadership as adults. Colleges and universities need to ask themselves today whether being able to analyze informational writings on honeybees should have equal or greater weight than being able to analyze C.S. Lewis warning against a subtle, dangerous temptation any college-educated student might face:

> We suspect that the bees of commercial bee colonies which are fed mono-crops are nutritionally deficient. In particular, we postulate that the problem is a diet deficient in anti-mite toxins: pyrethrums, and possibly other nutrients which are inherent in such plants.
>
> To nine out of ten of you the choice which could lead to scoundrelism will come, when it does come, in no very dramatic colors. Obviously bad men, obviously threatening or bribing, will almost certainly not appear. Over a drink, or a cup of coffee, disguised as triviality and sandwiched between two jokes, from the lips of a man, or woman, whom you have recently been getting to know rather better and whom you hope to know better still—just at the moment when you are most anxious not to appear crude, or naive, or a prig—the hint will come.

Standardized tests in the spirit of Newman and Sayers not only serve today's colleges well, but also promise to have an impact on the education offered by elementary and high schools. They will legitimize and reward the work of schools providing serious liberal arts education. Further, by featuring selections that witness to high moral and spiritual ideals, they break through a tyranny of indifference that continues to treat such ideals as merely private preferences at best, suspect sources of bias and hate at worst,[68] and consequently to undermine the ideals that our society so desperately needs today. As Tate says,

> The CLT is not a business idea. It is not a capitalist venture or another attempt at yet another educational fad. The CLT is a response to a national demand for values-based education, connecting knowledge with virtue.

---

[68] The aforementioned practice test includes a selection from Talleyrand, Minister of France, arguing that women should not receive a public education.

11

Welcome to the Future
Jeremy Tate[69]

Jeremy Tate is the founder and President of Classic Learning Initiatives. Jeremy is a graduate of Louisiana State University and Reformed Theological Seminary. Before founding Classic Learning Initiatives, Jeremy owned and operated an SAT prep company and served as a college counselor at Mount de Sales Academy in Catonsville, Maryland. Jeremy and his wife live in Annapolis, Maryland with their four children.

---

[69] This essay was originally published on September 23, 2016 at the John William Pope Center under the title "The SAT and ACT Fall Short, But Now There's a Better Alternative."

Parents, test prep experts, and college counselors, give careful thought in working with students as they approach the crucial "college entrance exam." Which of the two exams should they prep for? Which of the two exams will they do better on?

After running an SAT/ACT PREP company for a couple of years I became convinced the "SAT or ACT" question is even less important than "Coke or Pepsi? , "MAC or PC?" Anthony James-Green, test prep expert and "tutor to the 1 percent", argues that, "The new SAT, which launched on March 5th of 2016, is basically a carbon copy of the ACT – it was designed to be just that."[70]

These two testing giants, who now use tests of nearly identical content, also communicate a similar philosophy of education. For these two behemoths, it is all about "college and career readiness." In fact, the College Board, which creates the SAT, lists "college and career readiness" first when stating the purpose of the test.[71] But what is the purpose of college and a career? A nice paying job? A respectable title? Nicer stuff?

These questions are important as they ultimately shape the content of the test. The reading texts used in the SAT/ACT reflect that content doesn't matter. As Andrew Seeley stated in chapter ten, after reviewing a

---

[70] https://greentestprep.com/resources/sat-prep/new-sat-vs-act/
[71] https://collegereadiness.collegeboard.org/about/benefits

practice SAT, "One widely available practice test is dominated by selections that present information of little to no interest to anyone without a particular, momentary need, in language typical of textbooks or newspapers." Seeley goes on to list and describe numerous passages from the SAT and ultimately concludes that, "...high scores will be achieved by those who can analyze and edit such meaningless selections."

All testing is pedagogical. Tests teach. When logic, philosophy, theology, and ethics are missing from the most important test a student will take, students may reasonably conclude that these subjects simply don't matter. The SAT/ACT, as the ultimate tests and gateways to college, have a far bigger impact than a few lost Saturday mornings spent taking a meaningless test. These tests ultimately drive curriculum. Over the past year I have discussed the larger role of the SAT/ACT with dozens of headmasters and high school principals. They have relayed to me their conversations with parents and the pressure they are under to put students in front of the type of material they are most likely to see on the SAT/ACT.

The content of the SAT/ACT reflects an impoverished philosophy of education that stands in sharp contrast to the traditional or classical understanding of why we educate our children. For those in the western tradition, the formation of the human person—the formation of the heart in virtue—always stood paramount when considering the rationale for education. Plato put it this way: "The object of education is to teach us to love what is beautiful."

If developing virtue in our young people is the basic purpose of education, then the most important test they take in their young lives, the college entrance exam, should reflect this basic purpose as well. From Plato to John Quincy Adams, education meant formation in virtue. A "good education" meant a healthy dose of philosophy, logic, ethics, and theology. These disciplines have largely been removed from the public school arena. This removal, no doubt a partial result of their perceived uselessness on the SAT/ACT, has given birth to a generation that cries "bigotry" whenever someone suggests that perhaps tolerance isn't the only virtue.

Having been raised by a marine veteran from the Vietnam War, I knew the uselessness of pointing out problems without offering solutions. With this in mind, I wanted to create a solution by offering a third alternative for college entrance exams. In December of 2015 I co-founded the Classic Learning Test (CLT) with my lifetime best friend, business development expert and entrepreneur David Wagner. We launched the CLT with high hopes, but we have been shocked by the amount of enthusiasm traditionally minded educators and families have expressed towards the new test. The feedback we hear most often from families is simply, "we have been waiting for this."

Put simply, the CLT is an alternative to the SAT/ACT. The goal of the CLT, in tandem with everything we do as a company, is to reconnect intellectual pursuit and virtue. We believe that the ultimate testing standard, the college entrance exam, should be full of the greatest writers and thinkers in the history of western thought. From Aristotle to Immanuel Kant, the leaders of the western thought tradition have shared a profound concern for what classical educators refer to as "the good, the true, and the beautiful." The writers and thinkers students encounter when taking the CLT point them to the reality and existence of absolute truth, the sanctity of human life, and the irreplaceable value of personal character development.

Some thoughtful readers may react with skepticism. After all, we are talking about tests that a student only takes a couple of times, so how significant could an alternative be?

Shortly after launching the CLT, our team began receiving emails from parents asking the same question: "What type of curriculum would best prepare students for the CLT?" These emails confirmed our belief that college entrance exams drive curriculum in secondary schools. We realized that an alternative test could be influential enough to refocus secondary schools on the disciplines that shape the human heart. If a college entrance exam tests for ethical literacy, then students and parents will prepare accordingly. CLT tests have included passages from C.S. Lewis, G.K. Chesterton, Augustine, and Flannery O'Connor. The passages used engage the moral compass and conscience of a student rather than their intellect alone. As serious thinkers know, ideas have consequences; what people read shapes who they will become. Twenty years from now the measuring stick for the success of the CLT will not be found in the bottom line of corporate profits. Rather, the success of this endeavor will be gauged by the fruit it produces in the lives of the next generation and the degree to which it can contribute to a renaissance of virtue in America.

Appendix

Further References for Chapter 5

Americans for Educational Testing Reform. (2012). *Scorecard: ACT Inc.: Introduction.* Retrieved October 15, 2012, from http://aetr.org/the.facts/act

Cody, A. "Ranking and Sorting: The Sordid History of Standards and Tests" Living in Dialogue (website) http://www.livingindialogue.com/ranking-sorting-real-purpose-standards-tests/; accessed 2 Aug. 2016

Educational Testing Service. *ETS Builds a Test.* 1959. Princeton, New Jersey: Educational Testing Service, 1965.

Fancher, R. *The Intelligence Men: Makers of the IQ Controversy.* New York: W.W. Norton & Company, 1987

Fletcher, D. "Brief History: Standardized Testing." *Time* (website) December 11, 2009. http://content.time.com/time/nation/article/0,8599,1947019,00.html.

Grodsky, E., Warren, J., and Felts, E. "Testing and Social Stratification in American Education," *Annual Review of Sociology*, 34(2008), pp. 385-404.

Hoffman, B. *The Tyranny of Testing.* New York: Crowell-Collier Press, 1962.

Hout, M., and Elliott, S., Editors, *Incentives and Test-Based Accountability in Public Education*, National Research Council, National Academy of Sciences, 2011

Kamin, L. *The Science and Politics of I.Q.* Potomac, Md.: Lawrence Erlbaum Associates, 1974

Kuhn, T. *The Structure of Scientific Revolutions*, 3rd ed. (1962; Chicago, IL: University of Chicago Press, 1996).

Fletcher, Dan. *"Brief History: Standardized Testing".* 11 December 2009. <http://content.time.com/time/nation/article/0,8599, 1947019,00.html>.

Morse, R., Brooks, E., & Mason, M., at 9:36 p.m. *How U.S. News Calculated the 2016 Best Colleges Rankings.* 8 September Sept. 8, 2015. <http://www.usnews.com/education/best-colleges/articles/how-us-news-calculated-the-rankings>.

Reiss, J., and Sprenger, J. *"Scientific Objectivity,".* Summer 2016. <http://plato.stanford.edu/archives/sum2016/entries/scientific-objectivity/>.

Rooney, C. *Test Scores Do Not Equal Merit: Enhancing Equity & Excellence in College Admissions by Deemphasizing SAT and ACT Results.* Cambridge, MA: National Center for Fair & Open Testing, 1998.

SAT. *SAT Report on College and Career Readiness.* New York,
    NY: The College Board, 2013.

The National Center for Fair and Open Testing. *College
    Admissions Testing: The Real Beneficiaries.* 11 August
    2016. <http://fairtest.org/college-admissions-testing-
    real-beneficiaries>.